TADAS ZUKAS

Regulating Sustainable Finance in Europe

Regulating Sustainable Finance in Europe

By

Tadas Zukas

Duncker & Humblot · Berlin

Bibliografische Information der Deutschen Nationalbibliothek

Die Deutsche Nationalbibliothek verzeichnet diese Publikation in
der Deutschen Nationalbibliografie; detaillierte bibliografische Daten
sind im Internet über http://dnb.d-nb.de abrufbar.

Alle Rechte vorbehalten
© 2024 Duncker & Humblot GmbH, Berlin
Satz: L101 Mediengestaltung, Fürstenwalde
Druck: Books On Demand, Norderstedt
Printed in Germany

ISBN 978-3-428-19140-6 (Print)
ISBN 978-3-428-59140-4 (E-Book)

Gedruckt auf alterungsbeständigem (säurefreiem) Papier
entsprechend ISO 9706 ♾

Internet: http://www.duncker-humblot.de

Preface

The European Sustainable Finance Action Plan marked its 5th anniversary in 2023. Since its publication in 2018, the Action Plan reshaped the European sustainable finance. It has also substantially impacted the global sustainable finance debate. This remarkable document's first small round anniversary has served as our main reason for publishing this book at this point in time.

As I write these lines, the four key regulations that emerged out of the Action Plan's legislative agenda are now all in force (see *Figure*). The sustainable finance market is also in the process of reaching a new level of maturity in tackling greenwashing, which is also the European capital market supervisors' current strategic priority topic. And while there is some healthy debate ongoing among sustainable finance practitioners on whether the new European regulatory framework will be successful in practice, we are at the point of the sustainable finance regulatory journey where we can be reasonably certain regarding the direction it will take in the next five years. The new European regulatory architecture for sustainable finance is getting closer and closer to its conceptual completion.

Figure: The EU Action Plan – key regulations

The book that you hold in your hands is a reprint of my paper which has been originally published by Duncker & Humblot earlier this year as a contribution to an anniversary volume titled "Law and Economics in all its facets: Festschrift in Honor of Klaus Mathis", edited by Professor Peter Nobel, Alexander Gian-Carlo Baumann and Elias Aliverti.

We expect that the book format will make the text easier accessible to the broader sustainable finance expert community and will contribute to the European and global sustainable finance debate.

Zurich/Lucerne, November 2023 *Tadas Zukas*

Table of Contents

Preface		5
I.	Introduction	9
II.	Blueprint of the New Regulatory Architecture: The European Sustainable Finance Action Plan of 2018	12
	1. The Three Targets: Capital, Risk, Transparency	12
	2. The Ten Action Items: Reshaping the World of Finance	15
	3. Defining "Sustainable Finance"	18
	a) What Falls under "E", "S", "G"? The Action Plan's Guidance	19
	b) The Role of "G"	19
III.	Europe's Transparency and Anti-Greenwashing Regime: The Sustainable Finance Disclosure Regulation	22
	1. SFDR's Scope: Entities, Processes, Products	22
	2. "Let's Talk Sustainability": The Legislative Method	26
	3. Legislator's Purpose: Transparency and Anti-Greenwashing, Not Labelling	28
	a) Signal #1: Draft MiFID II Delegated Act on Sustainability Preferences (April 2021)	30
	b) Signal #2: SFDR/TR RTS Final Draft (April 2022)	31
	c) Signal #3: ESMA's Supervisory Briefing and Conference Notes (May 2022)	31
	4. Defining "Sustainable Investment"	33
	5. The Concept of "Sustainability Risk" and its Role	34
	6. Entity Level Sustainability Disclosures	37
	7. Financial Product Level Sustainability Disclosures	40
	a) Product-Level Sustainability Disclosures: The Strategy of Small Steps	40
	b) General Remarks on SFDR-Article-Product Categories	46
	8. Marketing Communications	51
IV.	Europe's "Green Vocabulary": The Taxonomy Regulation	52
	1. "Let's Get Technical"	52
	2. Defining "Environmentally Sustainable Investment"	53
	3. TR/SFDR Interplay	56
	4. TR/NFRD Interplay	59
V.	Centrality of Client's Choice: MiFID II and the New Duty to Inquire on Client's Sustainability Preferences	62

VI.	More Data for More ESG: The New Corporate Sustainability Reporting Directive	68
	1. Importance of Quality ESG Data for the Sustainable Finance Effort	68
	2. Context and Starting Point: NFRD's "Old" Corporate ESG Reporting Regime	69
	3. Laying the Foundation for CSRD: The Action Plan's "Fitness Check" of NFRD	70
	4. CSRD: Europe's New Corporate Sustainability Reporting Regime	72
VII.	Tackling Greenwashing	84
VIII.	Concluding Observations	90
List of References		93
Laws, Regulations, Official Documents		94

I. Introduction*

An invitation from the publishers to contribute a paper to this *Festschrift* volume celebrating the 55th anniversary and some of the most important career milestones of my esteemed colleague Professor Klaus Mathis of the University of Lucerne has been a true honour. As a law practitioner covering the area of sustainability regulation in my daily work, I feel tremendous admiration for the academic pioneers of this field of law such as Professor Mathis. Both the fact that Klaus Mathis holds the first law professorship concentrating on the law of the sustainable economy in Switzerland, as well as the fact that he has authored a major study, a 'habilitation' on the topic entitled "Sustainable development and inter-generational justice"[1], has served and continues to serve as a personal source of inspiration for focusing on sustainability and sustainable finance in particular in my career as a global business lawyer.

It would not be an overstatement to say that the topic of my paper – the European way of approaching the regulation of sustainable finance – is currently the hottest topic in finance regulation in Europe. A field of finance – known under various names such as "sustainable finance", "sustainable investing", "responsible investing", "green finance" and very often simply "sustainability" or just "ESG" (and sometimes misunderstood as a mere "check the box"-exercise) – which has been generally unregulated until very recently, is in process of becoming one of the most densely regulated areas in financial services. This primarily due to the European effort to address the field of sustainable finance which in the course of last years has been in process of constantly moving from a niche area to mainstream, a regulatory effort with an overarching aim to increase market transparency and efficiency, address sustainability risk and climate risk in particular and thus increase investor protection, channel private funds towards more sustainable economic activities and, very importantly, to prevent greenwashing.

---

* The author would wish to express a special thank you to Dr. Uwe Trafkowski, Frankfurt am Main, as well as to Dr. Egle Svilpaite, Lucerne/Zurich, for their comments on the initial draft of this paper. The views expressed in this paper are the author's personal views. The paper has been submitted for publication in August 2022; it has been updated in January 2023 to reflect the entry into force of CSRD and regulatory developments relating to greenwashing prevention.

[1] *Mathis*.

I. Introduction

Year (adoption)	Item / Go-live
2018	• European Sustainable Finance Action Plan • 8 March 2018
2019	• Sustainable Finance Disclosure Regulation (SFDR) • March 2021
2020	• Taxonomy Regulation (TR) • January 2022 / January 2023 (go-live key disclosure/reporting provisions)
2021	• MiFID II changes on sustainability preferences, other delegated acts • August 2022
2022	• SFDR/TR Level 2 • January 2023
2022	• Corporate Sustainability Reporting Directive (CSRD) • January 2024 (gradual go-live, first reporting in 2025)

Legend: Year indication on the left – adoption dates; dates on the right – go live dates key provisions.

Timeline overview: EU's emerging sustainable finance regulatory architecture – Key elements

This paper deals with the emerging regulatory architecture for sustainable finance in Europe, with various key concepts and pieces of it still being in flux and transition, their interplay in some parts still being open for conceptualization and (re)interpretation, on all levels. As the field of sustainable finance starts to dominate the practice of financial services regulation as no other, it is important to start conceptualizing it also on the academic level.

In order to fit the format set by the publishers, I will limit the scope of this contribution to asset and wealth management-related regulation, generally excluding insurance-related topics and other areas of finance. For the same reason, I will also focus on key elements of that new regulatory architecture, such as the Sustainable Finance Disclosure Regulation ("SFDR")[2], Taxonomy Regulation ("TR")[3], the Directive on Markets in Financial Instruments (MiFID II) regulatory framework changes regarding client's sustainability preferences as well as the Corporate Sustainability Reporting Directive

---

[2] Regulation (EU) 2019/2088 of the European Parliament and of the Council of 27 November 2019 on sustainability-related disclosures in the financial services sector, OJ L 317, pp. 1–16.

[3] Regulation (EU) 2020/852 of the European Parliament and of the Council of 18 June 2020 on the establishment of a framework to facilitate sustainable investment, and amending Regulation (EU) 2019/2088, OJ L 198, pp. 13–43.

("CSRD")[4], touching upon other topics from the European Union's current legislative pipeline in sustainable finance only briefly, to show their overall role and importance. Throughout the text, references to Europe are to be understood as referring to the European Union.

---

[4] Directive (EU) 2022/2464 of the European Parliament and of the Council of 14 December 2022 amending Regulation (EU) No 537/2014, Directive 2004/109/EC, Directive 2006/43/EC and Directive 2013/34/EU, as regards corporate sustainability reporting, OJ L 322, pp. 15–80.

II. Blueprint of the New Regulatory Architecture: The European Sustainable Finance Action Plan of 2018

In the course of the last few years, the amount, scope, density and pace of regulation in the field of sustainability and sustainable finance in particular has been increasing in a speed unseen before. In expert circles, the term of a regulatory tsunami in sustainable finance is sometimes used to describe this phenomenon. The political document which outlined the first grand contours of the vision of the new regulatory architecture for sustainable finance in Europe is the European Commission's communication dated 8 March 2018. It bears the official title of an "Action Plan: Financing Sustainable Growth", but is best known under its shorter title of the "Sustainable Finance Action Plan", and sometimes simply called an "Action Plan" or "EUAP".

1. The Three Targets: Capital, Risk, Transparency

The Sustainable Finance Action Plan aims to achieve the following three sustainability-related goals[1]:

1. *Reorienting capital flow*: in the European Commission's language, the Action Plan aims to "reorient capital flows towards sustainable investment in order to achieve sustainable and inclusive growth". This is the so-called *"inside-out perspective"* (considering how the firm's activities affect sustainability), which is new as a regulatory tool. In the document, the Commission points out that "current levels of investment are not sufficient to support an environmentally and socially sustainable economic system" and that there is a very substantial investment gap to close if the European Union wants to achieve its climate and energy 2030 targets. The Commission also identifies the circumstance of "lack of clarity among investors regarding what constitutes a sustainable investment" as a contributing factor behind the above-mentioned investment gap.[2]

2. *Improving financial risk management, integrating environmental and social risks*: "Manage financial risks stemming from climate change, resource depletion, environmental degradation and social issues". The requirement to include environmental and social goals in financial decision-

---

[1] Sustainable Finance Action Plan, p. 2.
[2] Sustainable Finance Action Plan, p. 2.

making aims to limit the financial impact of related environmental and social risks ("E/S risks"), such as the world's temperature increase of 2 degrees Celsius, which – in the European Commission's view – are currently "not always adequately taken into account by the financial sector." Climate change-related developments will mean that not only insurance companies experience higher disaster-related costs, but also banks financing companies most exposed to climate change or dependant on certain natural resources will be impacted.[3] Similar logic applies to social factors. This is the so-called *"outside-in perspective"* (considering how sustainability exposures affect the firm), which is typical for financial market regulation and various below discussed measures addressing it.

3. *Increasing market transparency, incentivising long-termism*: "Foster transparency and long-termism in financial and economic activity". Here, the Action Plan puts emphasis on the importance of market transparency for the purposes of a well-functioning financial system. Sustainability-related corporate transparency shall provide the markets with necessary information on their long-term viability and success. It shall also enable investors, including retail investors, to make better informed investment decisions. As the E&S-related investments require long-term orientation, which – according to the European Commission – are too often not supported by current short-time oriented market practices, the Commission expects to reduce those undue pressures for short-term performance in financial and economic decision-making by increasing transparency, which shall enable both corporate and retail investors to take better informed, more responsible decisions.[4]

In addition to these three general goals, on page 1 of the Action Plan, the European Commission states: "The EU is committed to *development that meets the needs of present and future generations*, while opening up new employment and investment opportunities and ensuring economic growth."[5] This note needs to be seen in context of the UN's definition of sustainable development as we know it from the UN's Brundtland Report (1987)[6], the Paris Agreement on climate change and the UN 2030 Agenda[7] including the 17 Sustainable Developments Goals (SDGs) to which the Action Plan refers right at the beginning of its considerations on the foundations of the Euro-

---

[3] Sustainable Finance Action Plan, p. 3.//
[4] Sustainable Finance Action Plan, p. 3.//
[5] Sustainable Finance Action Plan, p. 1.//
[6] UN Report of the World Commission on Environment and Development, Our Common Future, 1987.//
[7] UN General Assembly Resolution: Transforming our world: the 2030 Agenda for Sustainable Development, 25 September 2015, A/RES/70/1.

II. Blueprint of the New Regulatory Architecture

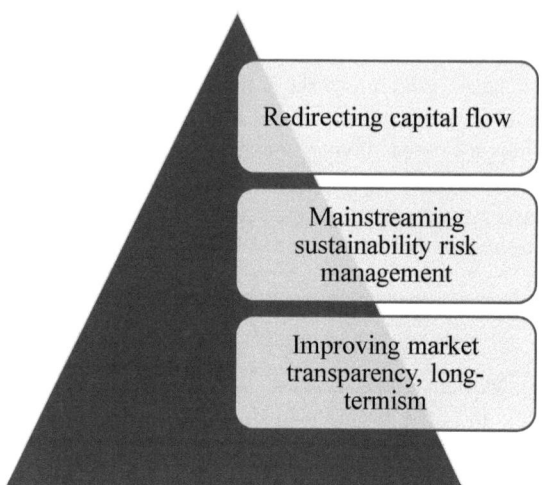

Figure: The three goals of the Sustainable Finance Action Plan 2018

pean sustainable finance effort.[8] It is the UN Brundtland Report which provides the globally accepted definition of sustainability/sustainability development, defining it as follows: *"Sustainable development is development that meets the needs of the present without compromising the ability of future generations to meet their own needs."*[9]

As we will dig deeper into details in the following chapters, it is important to keep these three general aims in mind. Not only will they prove to be helpful when putting each legislative action items in a broader context and connect it with others, it will also provide a good framework to conceptualize the field, which became so technical that there is a risk to get lost in details and lose focus on its post important aim of channelling more investments into sustainable economic activities.

It is important to keep the three goals in mind in order to remain aware that the Action Plan's legislative strategy has multiple layers, includes a sub-

---

[8] Sustainable Finance Action Plan, p. 1.

[9] UN Brundtland Report, p. 15, Section I (The Global Challenges), Sub-section 3 ("Sustainable Development"), Paragraph 27 ("Humanity has the ability to make development *sustainable to ensure that it meets the needs of the present without compromising the ability of future generations to meet their own needs*. The concept of sustainable development does imply limits – not absolute limits but limitations imposed by the present state of technology and social organization on environmental resources and by the ability of the biosphere to absorb the effects of human activities. But technology and social organization can be both managed and improved to make way for a new era of economic growth"). Emphasis added.

stantial level of complexity, and is not as one-dimensional and simplistic as sometimes portrayed.

2. The Ten Action Items: Reshaping the World of Finance

In the Action Plan, the European Commission proceeds very methodically in outlining its legislative agenda in sustainable finance and goes into a relatively high level of granularity when presenting legislative action items which shall help it to achieve its three aims. The planned actions are grouped around 10 action item clusters, which are as follows:

#	Sustainable Finance Action Plan: Action items
Action category 1: Reorienting capital flows towards sustainable investment	
1	Establishing an EU classification system for sustainable activities → Taxonomy Regulation (2020)
2	Creating standards and labels for green financial products
3	Fostering investment in sustainable projects
4	Incorporating sustainability when providing financial advice → MiFID II delegated act (2021)
5	Developing sustainability benchmarks
Action category 2: Mainstreaming sustainability into risk management	
6	Better integrating sustainability in ratings and market research
7	Clarifying institutional investors' and asset managers' duties
8	Incorporating sustainability in prudential requirements
Action category 3: Fostering transparency and long-termism	
9	Strengthening sustainability disclosure and accounting rule-making → SFDR (2019) → CSRD (2022)
10	Fostering sustainable corporate governance and attenuating short-termism in capital markets

As already mentioned, the term regulatory tsunami is increasingly used to describe the intensity of legislative and regulatory activity that has been triggered by the Action Plan and the ten action items. While all action items aim to address important aspects of the sustainable finance endeavour, certain legislative items are envisaged to play a particularly important role. Those will be the focus of my analysis in this paper.

II. Blueprint of the New Regulatory Architecture

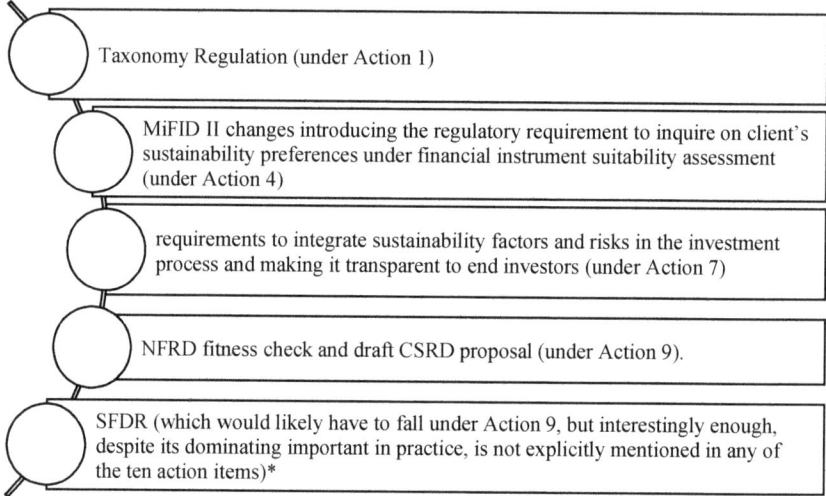

* Explanation: One of the reasons for that may be SFDR's broad scope spanning from financial products and advisory services, to corporate policies and reporting as well as marketing. It might also be its character as a "facilitator" for all other action items, if transparency and thus disclosures are understood as "the best of disinfectants." In the analysis that will follow, I will not only close this gap by analysing its requirements in detail, but also put it in proper context as central piece of the new European sustainable finance regulatory architecture.

Figure: Focus items – Sustainable Finance Action Plan

Very importantly, the Action Plan also provides some useful guidance in terms of political urgency and thus initial prioritization of the environmental aspects ("E"-topics) and the immediate need to address challenge of climate change in particular[10]:

"While the taxonomy work will begin on climate change mitigation, the scope will be progressively expanded to climate change adaptation and other environmental issues and, later, to social sustainability. Such an *approach reflects the urgency to act against climate change* and to meet our long-term climate and energy targets."

This initial focus on "E" and climate change in particular is a topic to which I will return later, as these are the topics more focus on which was required by the recent special report on ESG investing by The Economist[11].

---

[10] Sustainable Finance Action Plan, p. 11–12. Emphasis added.

[11] The Economist Special Report, see in particular the lead article "Three letters that won't save the planet: ESG should be boiled down to one simple measure: emissions", p. 7, and concluding article "The future of ESG: Measure less, but better – It's the environment, stupid", p. 12.

2. The Ten Action Items: Reshaping the World of Finance

The above listed focus items have reshaped the regulatory framework of finance regulation to an extent unseen before. In the next sections, we will focus on presenting, analysing and conceptualizing their content as well as interplay between the various action items in more detail, to show their unprecedented impact on the workings of the financial market in action.

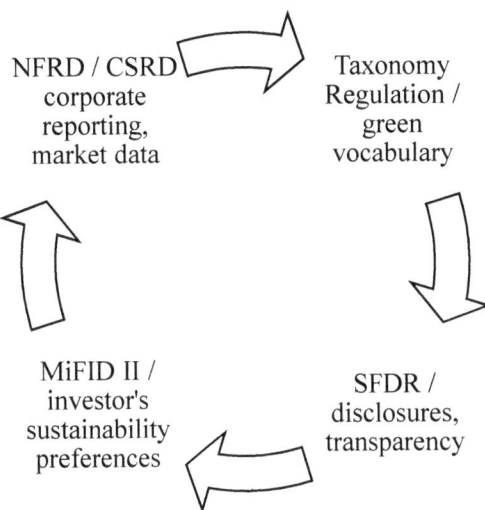

Figure: Interplay of key action items – Sustainable Finance Action Plan

In its new Sustainable Finance Strategy of 2021, the European Commission provides a useful overview of the interplay between key legislative action items under the new/envisaged European sustainable finance disclosure regime[12]:

---

[12] Sustainable Finance Strategy, p. 3.

EU sustainability disclosure regime for financial and non-financial companies			
Instrument	Corporate Sustainability Reporting Directive (CSRD)	Sustainable Finance Disclosure Regulation (SFDR)	Taxonomy Regulation
Scope	All EU large companies and all listed companies (except listed micro enterprises)	Financial market participants offering investment products, and financial advisers	Financial market participants; all companies subject to CSRD
Disclosure	Report on the basis of formal reporting standards and subject to external audit	Entity and product level disclosure on sustainability risks and principal adverse impacts	Turnover, capital and operating expenditures in the reporting year from products or activities associated with Taxonomy
Status	Applies from 2024	Applies from 10 March 2021	Applies from January 2022

Table source: Sustainable Finance Strategy 2021, p. 3 (updated to reflect adoption of CSRD).

In this context and for the sake of clarity, it needs to be added that the concept of investor's sustainability preferences and thus the centrality of client's choice as introduced with MiFID II delegated act's changes which started to apply in August 2022 play an essential role in the new EU's sustainable finance regulatory framework.

3. Defining "Sustainable Finance"

Clarity on definitions is of key importance for the sustainable finance effort. Different people mean different things when they speak of "sustainable finance." The Action Plan is of sure help here as it provides official guidance as to how the term needs to be understood in context of the new European sustainable finance regulatory architecture. The document not only defines the term and by doing so puts emphasis on its key elements. It also provides relatively detailed explanations on what exactly do the "E" (environmental considerations) and the "S" (social considerations) encompass, and also what role the "G" (governance) plays in the European Commission's regulatory thinking on the topic. The Action Plan defines sustainable finance as follows[13]:

---

[13] Sustainable Finance Action Plan, p. 2. Emphasis added.

3. Defining "Sustainable Finance"

"'Sustainable finance' generally refers to the *process* of *taking due account* of environmental *and* social considerations *in investment decision-making, leading to* increased investments in longer-term and sustainable activities."

Five key elements form the core of this definition: First, it's about the process and thus the definition is process-oriented; "sustainable development" may therefore be a better suitable term to understand the concept sustainable finance than the much used "sustainability" which is static. Second, sustainable finance is about "taking due account" of environmental *and* social considerations (the "E" and "S" in ESG). Third, the definition uses the "and" and not "or" when speaking about those considerations; it is an element of the definition which shall not be underestimated, not only for its conceptual importance, but also for its practical impact. It may be seen as a first indication under the Action Plan's logic that a contribution to either "E" or "S" alone is not enough to qualify an investment as sustainable, the other element – "E" or "S" respectively–needs to be properly taken into account. As we will see, this is exactly what is done when defining the test which needs to be passed under SFDR in order to qualify as "sustainable investment" under Art. 2(17) SFDR. The fourth important element clarifies the material scope of the definition: it speaks of "investment decision-making", the process of making investment decisions. While the first key element of the definition emphasized here makes clear that the definition of sustainable finance is process-oriented and may be understood by some as a pure "check the box"-exercise, the last, fifth element reminds us that that process is result oriented, functional: namely, it should lead to "investments in long-term and sustainable activities"[14].

a) What Falls under "E", "S", "G"? The Action Plan's Guidance

The Sustainable Finance Action Plan's section on the definition of sustainable finance provides some very useful details not only on what each of the letters in "ESG" encompasses content-wise (see figure below), but also some helpful insights on their interplay[15].

b) The Role of "G"

Particularly with regard to the content and role of "G" (governance) in "ESG", the Sustainable Finance Action Plan provides valuable guidance and insight into the European Commission's thinking on the topic. Especially for

---

[14] Sustainable Finance Action Plan, p. 2.
[15] Sustainable Finance Action Plan, p. 2.

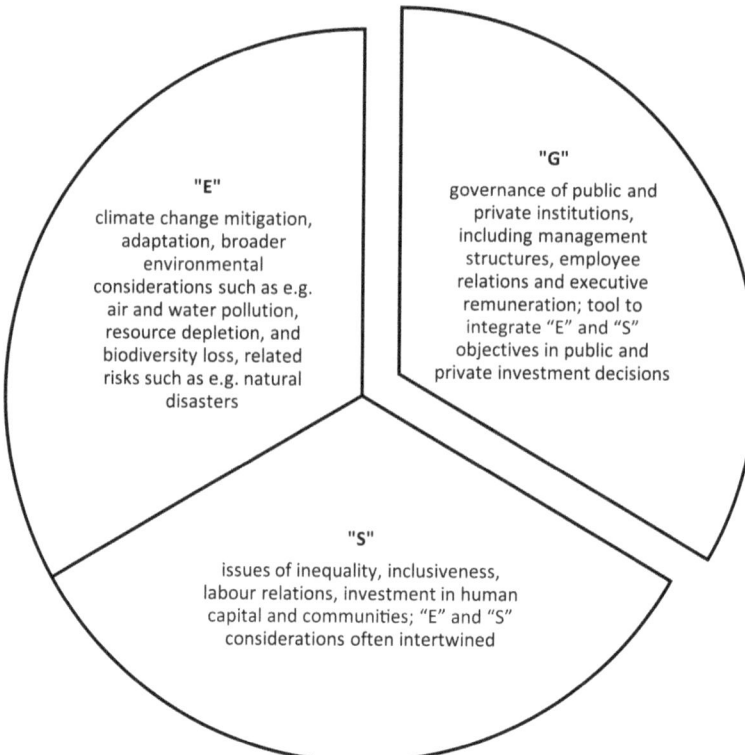

Figure: Core elements of "E", "S", "G" under the Sustainable Finance Action Plan

those seeing "G" as the core or even foundation of all ESG, the Action Plan not only includes considerations on what the "G" encompasses (see figure above), but also on the role it has in the interplay between "E" and "S." Looking at the content first, "G" is about "governance of public and private institutions, including management structures, employee relations and executive remuneration."[16] As for "G"'s role in context of broader ESG concept and sustainable finance in general, the Action Plan underscores an important point, namely that the "G" shall be seen not as a purpose in itself, but that it is a *"tool to integrate* environmental and social objectives in public and private investment decisions."[17] For example, as the Action Plan further explains, "executive compensation rules or incentives to protect shareholders'

---

[16] Sustainable Finance Action Plan, p. 2.
[17] Sustainable Finance Action Plan, p. 2. Emphasis added.

rights from managers are tools to ensure equality between the different stakeholders of a firm, i.e. managers, workers, shareholders and so on. In this case, in fighting inequality within a firm, governance performs a social goal." Listing of these items provides important practice guidance on where to start when considering to take the "G" in "ESG" seriously.

III. Europe's Transparency and Anti-Greenwashing Regime: The Sustainable Finance Disclosure Regulation

1. SFDR's Scope: Entities, Processes, Products

The SFDR – as the Sustainable Finance Disclosure Regulation is known in finance expert circles – addresses the field of sustainability in finance by targeting very specific aspects of it. It targets those aspects – as the name of the regulation itself as well the wording of Art. 1 SFDR defining the regulation's subject matter indicate – by using the instrument, or the tool, of transparency (thus the use of the term "disclosure" in the name and reference to "transparency" in its first article). In this context, it is very essential to understand that the SFDR is a transparency and anti-greenwashing regime, not a "labelling" regime – a topic to which we will discuss in more depth on the following pages. In terms of personal scope, the regulation addresses two types of financial market players: the "financial market participants" and "financial advisors" which are both regulatorily defined terms under the SFDR (see information boxes below). It sets regulatory requirements to them in the area of sustainability. More specifically, by requiring transparency regarding integration of sustainability risks and consideration of adverse sustainability impacts both on entity and process as well as financial product level. The SFDR provides for a regulatory definition of such key terms for the regulation's purpose as the "sustainability risk".[1] It also provides specific rules relating to transparency on sustainability characteristics of financial products. Last but certainly not least, the SFDR provides for a harmonized definition of the term "sustainable investment"[2], a key term in the entire sustainable finance and investing endeavour and debate. As a new regulatory market standard, this term is – just slightly more than a year after the regulation's entry into force – already in process of disciplining, if not revolutionizing, the sustainable finance practice.

---

[1] For further details on the concept of "sustainability risk" under SFDR, see Section III.5.

[2] For further details on the concept of "sustainable investment" under SFDR, see Section III.4.

1. SFDR's Scope

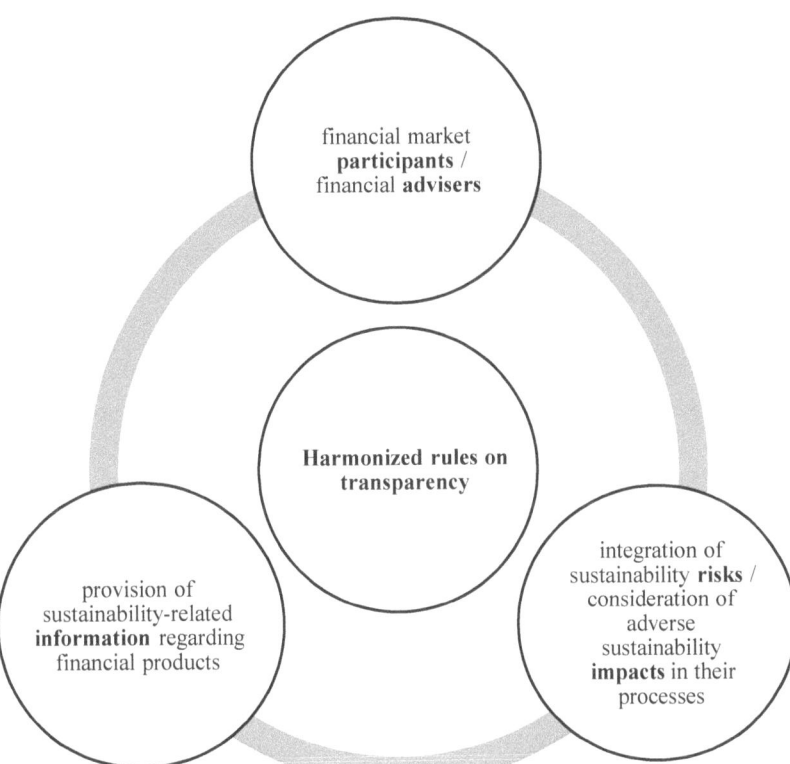

Figure: Overview – SFDR's subject matter

> **"Financial market participant" – SFDR's definition**
>
> **Art. 2(1) SFDR**
>
> 'financial market participant' means:
>
> (a) an insurance undertaking which makes available an insurance-based investment product (IBIP);
>
> (b) an investment firm which provides portfolio management;
>
> (c) an institution for occupational retirement provision (IORP);
>
> (d) a manufacturer of a pension product;
>
> (e) an alternative investment fund manager (AIFM);
>
> (f) a pan-European personal pension product (PEPP) provider;
>
> (g) a manager of a qualifying venture capital fund registered in accordance with Article 14 of Regulation (EU) No 345/2013;
>
> (h) a manager of a qualifying social entrepreneurship fund registered in accordance with Article 15 of Regulation (EU) No 346/2013;
>
> (i) a management company of an undertaking for collective investment in transferable securities (UCITS management company); or
>
> (j) a credit institution which provides portfolio management;

> **"Financial adviser" – SFDR's definition**
>
> **Art. 2(11) SFDR**
>
> 'financial adviser' means:
>
> (a) an insurance intermediary which provides insurance advice with regard to IBIPs;
>
> (b) an insurance undertaking which provides insurance advice with regard to IBIPs;
>
> (c) a credit institution which provides investment advice;
>
> (d) an investment firm which provides investment advice;
>
> (e) an AIFM which provides investment advice in accordance with point (b)(i) of Article 6(4) of Directive 2011/61/EU; or
>
> (f) a UCITS management company which provides investment advice in accordance with point (b)(i) of Article 6(3) of Directive 2009/65/EC;

1. SFDR's Scope

> **"Financial product" – SFDR's definition**
> **Art. 2(12) SFDR**
> 'financial product' means:
> (a) a portfolio managed* in accordance with point (6) of this Article;
> (b) an alternative investment fund (AIF);
> (c) an IBIP**;
> (d) a pension product;
> (e) a pension scheme;
> (f) a UCITS***; or
> (g) a PEPP****;
>
> Explanations:
> * 'portfolio management' means portfolio management as defined in point (8) of Article 4(1) of Directive 2014/65/EU, which states the following: "'portfolio management' means managing portfolios in accordance with mandates given by clients on a *discretionary client-by-client basis* where such portfolios include one or more *financial instruments*." Emphasis added.
> ** insurance-based investment product.
> *** undertaking for collective investment in transferable securities.
> **** pan-European personal pension product.

It is important to understand that the SFDR's scope is not limited to "financial products" and that it is also not limited "investment advice" relating to financial products as the term is defined under the SFDR. The regulation includes provisions which address investment advice in the broad sense as the term defined under MiFID II, which extends beyond investment advice on financial products as that term is defined under the SFDR. This conclusion can be derived from the definition of "investment advice" provided in Art. 2(16) SFDR (see information box below), which refers to MiFID II regulation's definition of the term. In the meantime, also the EU's regulatory authorities provided clarification and thus their point of view on this point.[3]

> **"Investment advice" – SFDR's definition**
> Art. 2(16) SFDR defines the investment advice by referring to MiFID II:
> (16) 'investment advice' means investment advice as defined in point (4) of Article 4(1) of Directive 2014/65/EU;
>
> **MiFID II definition of "investment advice"**
> Article 4(1)(4) of Directive 2014/65/EU defines the investment advice as follows:
> 'investment advice' means the provision of *personal recommendations* to a client, either upon its request or at the initiative of the investment firm, in respect of one or more transactions relating to financial instruments. Emphasis added.

---

[3] SFDR Q&A 5/2022, pp. 2, 4.

2. "Let's Talk Sustainability": The Legislative Method

As Recital 8 SFDR puts it, the European Union is "increasingly faced with the catastrophic and unpredictable consequences of climate change, resource depletion and other sustainability-related issues, urgent action is needed to mobilise capital not only through public policies but also by the financial services sector." As one of important measures to address this urgency and problem, the EU chose not generally prohibiting certain unsustainable practices in finance, but increasing market transparency and thus awareness on those, accompanied by an expectation or hope that this would likely lead to market's self-correction, based on more market information made available thanks to regulatory disclosure obligations. Following this line of thinking, the SFDR now requires financial market participants and financial advisers to "disclose specific information regarding their approaches to the integration of sustainability risks and the consideration of adverse sustainability impacts" (Recital 8). Here, the European Union seems to take a general assumption as a starting point in its regulatory endeavour that information asymmetries on sustainability-related questions exist between the financial market participants and financial advisors on one hand (as agents) and the end investors on the other (principals) and that removing those would improve the functioning of the market, nudge its players towards investments into more sustainable economic activities. And so, accordingly, what the SFDR aims at "by requiring financial market participants and financial advisers to make pre-contractual and ongoing disclosures to end investors when they act as agents of those end investors (principals)", is to not simply add an additional administrative check-the-box burden on the market players, but "to reduce information asymmetries in principal-agent relationships with regard to the integration of sustainability risks, the consideration of adverse sustainability impacts, the promotion of environmental or social characteristics, and sustainable investment" (Recital 10).

When addressing the sustainability risk integration, the SFDR generally leaves it up to the financial market players to judge for themselves if sustainability risks are of relevance to them and their product and service offerings. What the SFDR aims to achieve with this regulatory approach is creating market transparency on the market players' approaches to the question of integrating sustainability risks. As Recital 15 SFDR puts it, "[w]here the sustainability risk assessment leads to the conclusion that there are no sustainability risks deemed to be relevant to the financial product, the reasons therefor should be explained. Where the assessment leads to the conclusion that those risks are relevant, the extent to which those sustainability risks might impact the performance of the financial product should be disclosed either in qualitative or quantitative terms." Recital 15 SFDR further describes the information flow on the topic from market participants to financial advisers: "The sustainability risk assessments and related pre-contractual disclosures by financial market participants should feed into pre-contractual disclosures by financial advisers". And, via the financial advisers, to clients: "Financial advisers should disclose how they take sustainability risks into account in the selection process of the financial product that is presented to the end investors before providing the advice, *regardless of the sustainability preferences of the end investors*" (emphasis added). This last aspect that sustainability risks shall be made topic of conversation also with clients having no particular sustainability preferences is sometimes still underestimated and so is its practical importance.

The European legislator's approach under SFDR can be summarized as requiring the financial market players make their stand on sustainability risk and adverse sustainability impacts public and provide explanations if they consider those risks not relevant. *"Comply or explain"* may be a slight simplification describing this approach, but it in fact reflects the core of legislator's approach. It is of paramount importance to understand that the SFDR requires to say what you as a regulated subject in fact do; it does not generally require something more than this. In its essence, the SFDR's regulatory approach is an approach of mandated disclosures, a legal concept or insight that we know for more than 100 years in the form of US Justice's Brandeis insightful observation: "Sunlight is said to be the best of disinfectants".[4]

The SFDR asks the financial market participants and financial advisers to put their "talk" about sustainability in formal pre-contractual client documents and periodic reports, but also make that "talk" available via website channel. With the market not correctly interpreting the SFDR in the initial phase of its rollout as a "labelling regime" seeing SFDR-Article 6, 8, 9-Products as "sustainability labels" and thus jumping onto that "invitation" to formalize the sustainability-related talk and this way flooding the market with sustainability-related statements, the regulator may have already achieved more than anyone may have expected for this short period of time since SFDR's go-live date in March 2021.

---

[4] *Brandeis*, p. 92. For the general criticism of that approach under the US law see *Ben-Shahar/Schneider*.

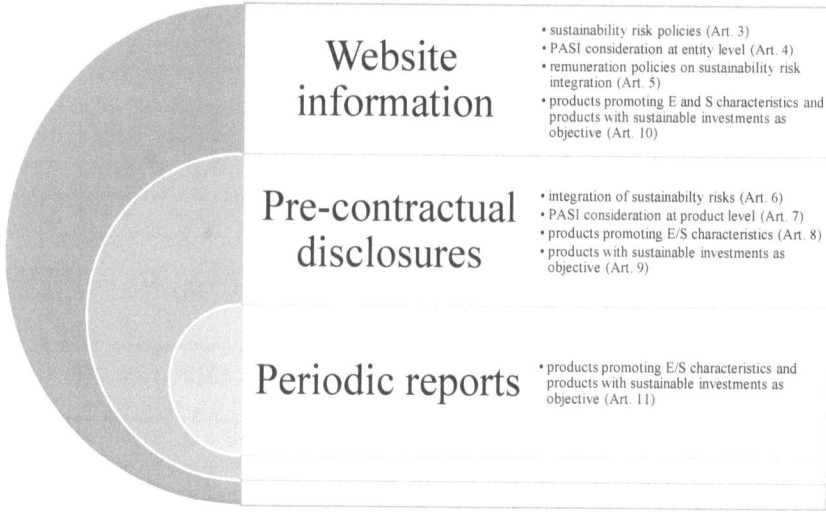

Legend: "PASI" – Principal adverse sustainability impacts; "E" – environmental; "S" – social.

Overview – Transparency obligations and channels under SFDR

3. Legislator's Purpose: Transparency and Anti-Greenwashing, Not Labelling

The title of the regulation, the Sustainable Finance *Disclosure* Regulation, speaks for itself: it's a disclosure regulation, a regulation on "sustainability-related *disclosures* in the financial services sector" (emphasis added).[5] Its first provision outlining the regulation's subject matter reemphasizes this point in other words by stating that the regulation is about sustainability-related *"transparency"* (Art. 1 SFDR). Basically, all SFDR disclosure provisions are structured in such a way that they contribute to making lives of potential "green washers" as difficult as possible on both entity as well as product levels.[6] It is for this reason that the SFDR is sometimes also called Europe's anti-greenwashing regime in sustainable finance.

Recital 10 SFDR clarifies what the primary purpose of those transparency duties is:

"This Regulation *aims to reduce information asymmetries* in principal-agent relationships with regard to the integration of sustainability risks, the consideration of

---

[5] Regulation (EU) No 2019/2088 of the European Parliament and of the Council of 27 November 2019 on sustainability-related disclosures in the financial services sector ("SFDR"), OJ L 317, pp. 1–16.

[6] *Zukas/Trafkowski*, p. 20.

adverse sustainability impacts, the promotion of environmental or social characteristics, and sustainable investment, *by requiring* financial market participants and financial advisers *to make pre-contractual and ongoing disclosures to end investors* when they act as agents of those end investors (principals)." (Emphasis added)

In addition to those general disclosure requirements, the regulation includes a dedicated provision specifically addressing the field of organisations' activities traditionally associated with the highest risk of greenwashing exposure, which is marketing communications. That provision is Art. 13 SFDR, which states that "financial market participants and financial advisers shall ensure that their marketing communications *do not contradict the information disclosed* pursuant to this Regulation". It is sometimes described as a basic anti-greenwashing provision under SFDR's regulatory regime.

It is very essential to understand that the SFDR is a transparency and anti-greenwashing regime, not a "labelling" regime. While this observation might look as something self-evident today, it has not been so from the beginning of SFDR's go-live date. It is an interesting practical phenomenon and development illustrating the factual force of market dynamics, which has been addressed by ESMA's chair Verena Ross in her speech at a funds industry conference in May 2022[7]:

> "While SFDR was designed to enhance transparency around sustainability, we have noted that in practice the disclosures are often being used as *product classification*. Status as 'Article 8' or 'Article 9' funds are being used in marketing material by fund managers as *quality labels for sustainability*."

This observation can be seen as culmination of European authorities' efforts over more than a year since SFDR's go-live on 10 March 2021 to make this point and raise market awareness of it. The below list gives an overview of the respective timeline and key official sources regarding this effort (see figure next page).

The circumstance that the market seems to be still somewhat puzzled about this point may raise questions why it is so. One of the reasons for that may be the complexity of the entire Sustainable Finance Action Plan's legislative effort and the interconnectedness and interplay between its various items, which may still be not fully understood in all its conceptual depth by all market players. The following sections give a more in-depth overview as the regulatory efforts aimed at signalling the message on SFDR's purpose and the slowly establishing that view by correcting the view held by large segments of the ESG market.

---

[7] *Ross*, p. 7. Emphasis added.

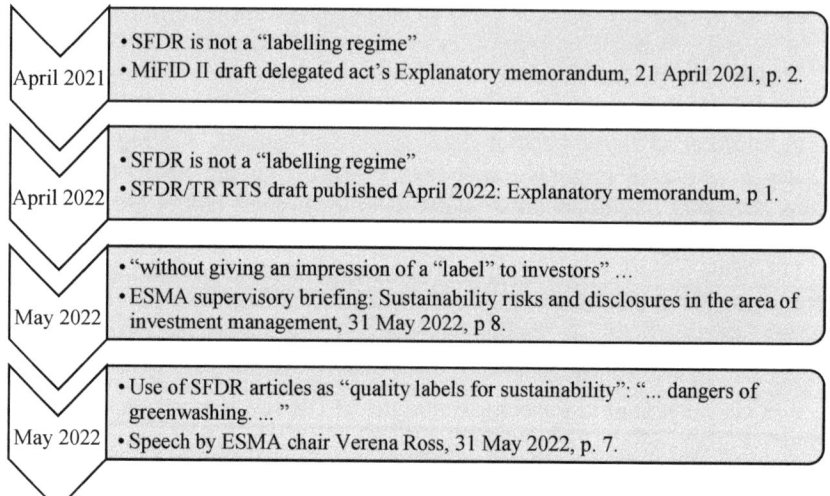

Timeline overview: SFDR is "not a labelling regime" – clarification efforts

a) Signal #1: Draft MiFID II Delegated Act on Sustainability Preferences (April 2021)

The effort to clarify the point that SFDR is not a labelling regime has started in an unexpected place for some: the draft MiFID II delegated act's on sustainability preferences Explanatory memorandum of 21 April 2021[8]. Looking back, that sustainability preferences-related document seems to have been intended to become a true game changer for the SFDR experts in the sense that it made them realize that none of the SFDR-article-product-categories would per se qualify as being eligible as fulfilling clients' sustainability preferences in accordance with the upcoming MiFID II regulatory regime. In other words, the memorandum, as well as the draft legislative provisions of MiFID II on sustainability preferences that it accompanied, made clear that it is not the concepts of Art. 6, 8 or 9 SFDR that will play a decisive role under Europe's new sustainable finance regulatory architecture, particularly for purposes of MiFID II sustainability preferences, but the substance/materiality-oriented provisions such as Art. 2(17) SFDR defining what "sustainable investment" is, Art. 2(1) Taxonomy Regulation defining what "environmentally sustainable investment" is and, lastly but not least importantly, the category of financial instruments/products considering principle adverse sustainability impacts ("PASI"). This last preference category bears resemblance to the PASI concept

---

[8] MiFID II delegated act's draft, April 2021, p. 2.

under Art. 4 SFDR (PASI consideration at entity level) and Art. 7 SFDR (PASI consideration at financial product level), though these two SFDR provisions are not explicitly referred to in the new wording of MiFID II. This observation in MiFID II's Explanatory memorandum started to show first influences on some conceptual SFDR expert debates, especially in context of, or in combination with the EC's SFDR Q&A of July 2021, which made clear that the fact of mere sustainability risk integration is not sufficient to trigger Art. 8 SFDR disclosure obligations and thus qualify the respective product as "promoting" sustainability characteristics[9], it took some time for the argument and insight to gain more traction even in the expert circles focusing on the SFDR implementation.

b) Signal #2: SFDR/TR RTS Final Draft (April 2022)

With the publication of the final draft of SFDR/TR RTS in April 2022, the point that SFDR is *"not a labelling regime"* was made very clear also directly in the SFDR context.[10] It is in this document that the fight against greenwashing has been emphasized even clearer in the SFDR context by stating that SFDR's aim is not only to "improve sustainability-related disclosures, comparability of the disclosures for end investors", but also to reduce "the occurrence of adverse sustainability impacts *and greenwashing*."[11]

Some of the well-known global law firms with particular expertise in sustainable finance regulation such as Simmons & Simmons noted this development and commented it in some detail in their public client note, which also shared the firm's expert observations on the *market practice that diverges from this view* and that the market would likely see this "development" as an unwelcome one.[12]

c) Signal #3: ESMA's Supervisory Briefing and Conference Notes (May 2022)

European authorities' signalling on the point that SFDR is not a labelling regime continued on a more technical level in May 2022. ESMA's supervisory briefing on "Sustainability risks and disclosures in the area of investment management" touched upon the point an a rather indirect manner, by observing that product classification should be conducted *"without giving an impres-*

---

[9] SFDR Q&A 7/2021, p. 8.
[10] SFDR/TR RTS final draft 4/2022, Explanatory Memorandum, p. 1.
[11] SFDR/TR RTS final draft 4/2022, Explanatory Memorandum, p. 1. Emphasis added.
[12] *Simmons & Simmons*, pp. 1, 3.

sion of a 'label' to investors".[13] ESMA's concerns regarding this point were made public in a much more detailed manner in a speech by ESMA chair Verena Ross, delivered on 31 May 2022 at a fund industry's conference in Dublin, putting those concerns in context of the greenwashing risk topic[14]:

> "... Going beyond the design of the rules, I would like to add a few words on their actual application and the *dangers of greenwashing*. While SFDR was designed to enhance transparency around sustainability, we have noted that in practice the disclosures are often being *used as product classification*. Status as 'Article 8' or 'Article 9' funds are being used in marketing material by fund managers *as quality labels for sustainability*. We are particularly concerned for investors investing in products disclosing under Article 8 SFDR.
>
> It is important to remember that the purpose of Article 8 disclosures is to highlight any kind of environmental or social characteristics promoted by such products – however small it might be. It is therefore very *important that investors do not take the mere presence of an Article 8 disclosure as an indication of sustainability per se.* ..."

Implications of this interpretational clarification on SFDR's role and function in the new European sustainable finance regulatory architecture are yet in process of being properly absorbed by the market. Properly understanding the point that SFDR is not a labelling, but a transparency and anti-greenwashing regime makes it clearer why no thresholds for Art. 8 or 9 SFDR products are set by the legislator, a question which has occupied the minds of many sustainable finance practitioners from the very beginning of the SFDR project. It also helps returning the substantive focus to the other, materiality-oriented SFDR's and Taxonomy Regulation's provisions: While Article 6 and particularly Art. 8 and Art. 9 SFDR disclosures play a key procedural role in reaching the Sustainable Finance Action Plan's and SFDR's as its transparency regime's purposes, it is not these provisions that will play a substance/materiality-focused role in sustainable finance endeavour, but Art. 2(17) SFDR (definition of "sustainable investment"), Art. 2(1) Taxonomy Regulation (definition of "environmentally sustainable investment") and, indirectly, Articles 4 and 7 SFDR (consideration of PASI on entity and product levels).[15] This interpretational correction of establishing market practices by Europe's regulators also makes clear that focusing on details and not understanding grand purpose of a regulation may lead to creating greenwashing risks by giving an incorrect impression that SFDR article products are "quality labels" for sustainability. It is obviously of key importance to understand this aspect to properly navigate the new European sustainable finance regulatory architecture in general. But it is also of essential importance to understand this point in order to not trigger additional

---

[13] ESMA's supervisory briefing 5/2022, p. 8. Emphasis added.
[14] *Ross*, p. 7. Emphasis added.
[15] Explanatory memorandum to MiFID II delegated act's draft, April 2021, p. 2.

greenwashing risks by creating an impression in clients' eyes that SFDR-article-product categories are per se quality labels for sustainability. For in-house legal departments, the even deeper lesson-learned in this context may be to not underestimate the importance of fundamental legal interpretation skills, the importance of independent in-house legal analysis of new regulatory concepts and thus also the importance of in-house legal capabilities for the purpose of enabling financial institutions' to properly navigate the regulatory business transformation challenges posed by the ever more fast-paced and increasingly complex regulatory landscape.

4. Defining "Sustainable Investment"

We explained in Section III.3. that SFDR is not a labelling, but a transparency and anti-greenwashing regime. We also made clear that when it comes to the substance of what qualifies as "sustainable", it is not the disclosure-focused provisions of Art. 6, 8 or 9 SFDR which play central role in defining that, but the initially not so "prominent" technical provision of Art. 2(17) SFDR.

As part of regulatory agenda driven by the regulation's legislative purpose referred to in Art. 1 SFDR to set harmonized rules for sustainable finance, the SFDR provides a definition of the term "sustainable investment." The SFDR's ambition to lay down such harmonized definition of this term is emphasized in Recital 17 SFDR:

> "To ensure the coherent and consistent application of this Regulation, it is necessary to lay down a harmonised definition of 'sustainable investment' ..."

The definition of what qualifies as "sustainable investment" under SFDR's regulatory framework is provided in Art. 2 SFDR, which is dedicated to the SFDR's vocabulary and key sustainable finance definitions. It reads as follows:

"Sustainable investment" – SFDR's definition

Art. 2(17) SFDR

'sustainable investment' means an investment in an economic activity that *contributes* to an *environmental* objective, as measured, for example, by key resource efficiency indicators on the use of energy, renewable energy, raw materials, water and land, on the production of waste, and greenhouse gas emissions, or on its impact on biodiversity and the circular economy, *or* an investment in an economic activity that *contributes* to a *social* objective, in particular an investment that contributes to tackling inequality or that fosters social cohesion, social integration and labour relations, or an investment in human capital or economically or socially disadvantaged communities, *provided that* such investments *do not significantly harm* any of those objectives and that the investee companies *follow good governance* practices, in particular with respect to sound management structures, employee relations, remuneration of staff and tax compliance. (emphasis added)

Not only does the definition list the key elements forming the core of what qualifies as "sustainable investment", it also provides some level of detail as to what each of those elements entail. While some uncertainties as to exact meaning of those elements may remain until the relevant supervisory and market practice develops, it can be said already at this stage that clarity on such key definition will help the effort to differentiate which investments qualify as sustainable and which not. The definition also plays a key role in Art. 8 and 9 SFDR disclosures, which ask to identify proportion of investments which qualify as sustainable investments under the SFDR Level 2 templates.

The key elements of SFDR's Art. 2(17) definition of "sustainable investment" can be shown by using the following figure:

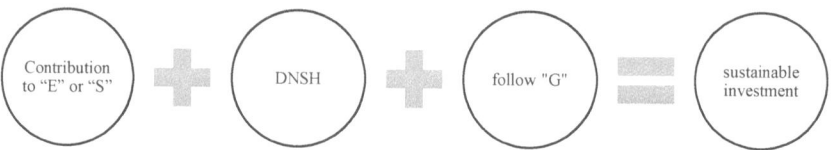

Legend: "E" – environmental objective; "S" – social objective; "G" – good governance; "DNSH" – do no significant harm.

Figure: "Sustainable investment" under SFDR – key elements

5. The Concept of "Sustainability Risk" and its Role

Addressing the topic of sustainability risk and increasing transparency on how financial market players deal with them is at the core of SFDR's purpose, as clearly indicated in Art. 1 SFDR. Numerous other SFDR provisions address the topic. It is therefore of essential importance how the concept of "sustainability risk" shall be understood under SFDR and what the legislator aims to address when setting out rules requiring to disclose how a financial market player deals with the sustainability risk.

The above explained considerations in Section III.3. on SFDR's purpose and the circumstance that it is not a labelling regime also have an impact on proper understanding of sustainability risk integration-related SFDR provisions. These are primarily disclosure-oriented provisions, which may help understanding why the mere fact of sustainability risk integration by a financial product as per Art. 6 SFDR does not only not trigger Art. 8 SFDR disclosure regime[16], but also – naturally – does not suffice to classify that product as "sustainable".

---

[16] SFDR Q&A 7/2021, p. 8.

5. The Concept of "Sustainability Risk" and its Role

How the term "sustainability risk" shall to be understood in context of Europe's new sustainable finance regulatory framework is defined in Art. 2(22) SFDR, which reads as follows:

> **"Sustainability risk" – SFDR's definition**
> **Art. 2(22) SFDR**
> 'sustainability risk' means an environmental, social or governance *event or condition* that, if it occurs, could cause an actual or a potential *material negative impact* on the *value of the investment*; (emphasis added)

The definition is technical, it is rather narrow in its character and focused on "material negative impact on the value of the investment" that an ESG "event or condition", if it occurs, could cause. For the proper implementation of sustainability risk integration requirements under the SFDR, it is essential to understand that definition's narrow focus. Seeing climate risk as the currently most important sub-category of sustainability risk, realization of one or another climate change scenario development could qualify as an "event or condition" in the sense of Art. 2(22) SFDR.

The following SFDR provisions set explicit requirements on sustainability risk integration and disclosure:

SFDR-Art.	Art.-Title	Topic/Requirement	Transparency channel
General			
Art. 1	Subject matter	– "integration of sustainability risks" ("in their processes") ➔ Applicable to both financial market participants and financial advisers	General requirement
Art. 2(22)	Definitions	Harmonized definition of "sustainability risk"	General requirement
Organisation/Processes			
Art. 3(1)	Transparency of sustainability risk policies	– "integration of sustainability risks" in *investment decisions* ➔ Applicable to financial market participants	Website publication of required information
Art. 3(2)	Transparency of sustainability risk policies	– "integration of sustainability risks" in *investment advice* ➔ Applicable to financial advisers	Website publication of required information

SFDR-Art.	Art.-Title	Topic/Requirement	Transparency channel
Art. 5	Transparency of remuneration policies in relation to the integration of sustainability risks	– "integration of sustainability risks" in *remuneration policies* ➔ Applicable to both financial market participants and financial advisers	Website publication of required information
Products & services			
Art. 6(1)	Transparency of the integration of sustainability risks	– manner of integrating sustainability risks in *investment decisions* and – *impact* of sustainability risks on their products' *returns* ➔ Applicable to financial market participants	Pre-contractual disclosure
Art. 6(2)	Transparency of the integration of sustainability risks	– manner of integrating sustainability risks in *investment advice* and – *impact* of sustainability risks on *returns* of products they advise on ➔ Applicable to financial advisers	Pre-contractual disclosure
Art. 6(1)–(2)	Transparency of the integration of sustainability risks	– if *considered not relevant* – reasons therefor ("Comply or explain") ➔ Applicable to both financial market participants and financial advisers	Pre-contractual disclosure

Overview: SFDR requirements – transparency on sustainability risk integration

Despite the importance of the topic, sustainability risk topic remains to be somewhat overshadowed by other SFDR-related themes such as product qualification, definition of sustainable investment, disclosure contents and channels, requirements for marketing communications and such topics as greenwashing. Proper management of sustainability risk shall be considered part of good risk management and it also adds value to clients, also those with no sustainability preferences. The European Commission's important clarification that integrating sustainability risks per se does not trigger disclosure obligations of Art. 8 SFDR[17], can generally be interpreted as meaning that information on sustainability risk integration can, if done carefully and in a disciplined manner, be provided without triggering the extensive Art. 8 SFDR disclosure obligations.

Art. 6 SFDR on sustainability risk integration transparency at financial product level can also be seen as a "reference" provision for Art. 8 and 9 SFDR product disclosures as both of these base their disclosure regime by referring to Art. 6 SFDR. In this context, it should be made clear that also the category of Art. 6 SFDR products stating that they do not integrate sustainability risks can trigger the Art. 8 SFDR disclosure regime if they use language qualifying as "promotion" of E/S characteristics under that requirement. It needs to be noted that a further enhancement of regulatory requirements on the sustainability risk topic has been added by the "Sustainable Finance April Package" of 2021, most of which started to apply in August 2022.[18]

6. Entity Level Sustainability Disclosures

While the current market debate is strongly focused on SFDR's financial product related disclosures, the entity level sustainability disclosures (though very technical and addressed more to professionals that regular investors) play not lesser role under the SFDR's transparency regime. The relevant provision setting out the requirements for entity level disclosures is Art. 4 SFDR ("Transparency of adverse sustainability impacts at entity level"). As the title of this provision indicates, the norm focuses on the concept of "adverse sustainability impacts", i.e. reducing negative externalities[19] or "negative effects on sustainability factors"[20].

The provision requires entities in scope of Art. 4 SFDR to disclose *on their websites* whether they consider adverse sustainability impacts. Those disclosures shall not only be published on the website in accordance to a regulatory predefined template, but they also need to be constantly maintained. Art. 4 SFDR uses the *"comply or explain"-mechanism* for this purpose, which is used in setting the requirement for both financial market participants and financial advisors.

---

[17] SFDR Q&A 7/2021, p. 8.
[18] European Commission, Communication, Sustainable Finance Package, 21 April 2021 (available at: <https://ec.europa.eu/info/publications/210421-sustainable-finance-communication_en>, last visited on January 15, 2023).
[19] SFDR Q&A 7/2021, p. 3.
[20] Recital 20, last sentence, SFDR.

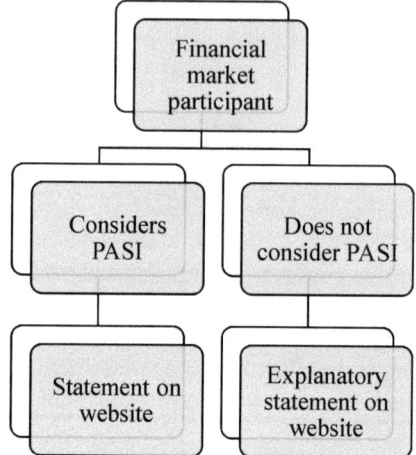

Legend: PASI stands for "principal adverse sustainability impacts", which is an abbreviation for the SFDR's concept "principal adverse impacts of investment decisions on sustainability factors". Note that this "comply of explain"-mechanism does not apply to financial market participants of certain size as per Art. 4(3) and Art. 4(4) SFDR, which shall publish PASI statements mandatorily.

Figure: Overview – PASI statement requirements for financial market participants

Art. 4 SFDR sets requirements for both types of PASI statements to be made by the **financial market participants**:

Financial market participants which *consider* principal adverse impacts of investment decisions on sustainability factors, need to publish and maintain on their website a statement "on due diligence policies with respect to those impacts, taking due account of their size, the nature and scale of their activities and the types of financial products they make available" (see Art. 4(1)(a) SFDR).

Financial market participants which *do not consider* principal adverse impacts of investment decisions on sustainability factors, need to publish and maintain on their website an explanatory statement with "clear reasons for why they do not do so, including, where relevant, information as to whether and when they intend to consider such adverse impacts" (see Art. 4(1)(b) SFDR).

For the financial market participants which consider PASI, the SFDR sets standardized minimum requirements for the PASI statement ("include … at least the following"), which are outlined in Art. 4(2) SFDR:

– information about their policies on the identification and prioritisation of principal adverse sustainability impacts and indicators;

6. Entity Level Sustainability Disclosures

– a description of the principal adverse sustainability impacts and of any actions in relation thereto taken or, where relevant, planned;
– brief summaries of engagement policies in accordance with Article 3g of Directive 2007/36/EC, where applicable;
– a reference to their adherence to responsible business conduct codes and internationally recognised standards for due diligence and reporting and, where relevant, the degree of their alignment with the objectives of the Paris Agreement.

Furthermore, Art. 4(3) and Art. 4(4) SFDR, from 30 June 2021, exclude the possibility to "opt out" from entity-level PASI reporting for a category of financial market *participants* of certain size, using the criterion of the average number of 500 employees during the financial year for this purpose.

In addition to this, the Level 2 act to SFDR, its which went into force per January 2023 sets technical and very detailed requirements on entity level PASI statement, which will need to be made following predefined template as per Annex 1 to the SFDR Level 2 act.

For both types of PASI statements to be made by the **financial advisers**, Art. 4 SFDR sets requirements which are considerably less detailed and technical than the ones set for financial market participants. The financial advisers shall publish and maintain on their websites the following information:

– "information as to whether, taking due account of their size, the nature and scale of their activities and the types of financial products they advise on,

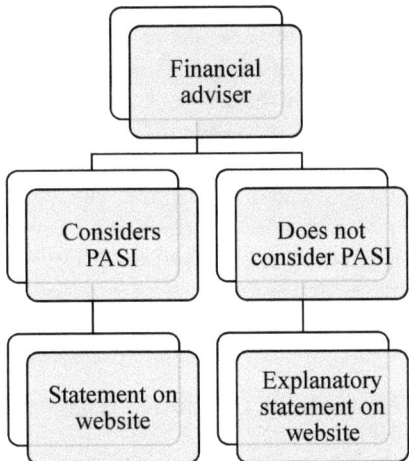

Figure: Overview – PASI statement requirements for financial advisers

they consider in their investment advice or insurance advice the principal adverse impacts on sustainability factors"; or

– "information as to why they do not to consider adverse impacts of investment decisions on sustainability factors in their investment advice or insurance advice, and, where relevant, including information as to whether and when they intend to consider such adverse impacts".

In addition to this, the Level 2 act to SFDR, which went into force in January 2023, sets additional technical requirements on entity level PASI statement to be published by the financial advisers. These are by far not as detailed as the ones foreseen for the financial market participants. It also needs to be noted that there are no comparable special rules for large financial advisers as those stipulated in Art. 4(3) and Art. 4(4) SFDR, which are addressed to financial participants.

7. Financial Product Level Sustainability Disclosures

The extensive financial product level disclosure requirements introduced by the Sustainable Finance Disclosure Regulation certainly form a core of the SFDR regulation, especially as it relates to its impact on the market practice. In its approach to product level disclosures, the SFDR proceeds with a strategy, which may be described as a strategy of small steps, or a strategy of gradual expansion, intensification of product-related sustainability disclosures. SFDR Articles 6-7-8-9 perhaps can be best understood as gradual steps revealing financial market participant's approach to sustainability at the financial product level. As discussed above in Section III.3., it is important to understand that SFDR article categories are not "labels" and not "sustainability labels". The purpose of those SFDR articles is to get the information to the market on the financial market participants' approach to sustainability as relates to their products, and especially "catch" the financial products making any sustainability-related claims into the disclosure framework so that those claims can be scrutinized using SFDR's concepts such as the definition of "sustainable investment" as well as SFDR's standardized periodic reporting requirements, which are requirements intended to make the lives of potential green washers as difficult and inconvenient as possible.

a) Product-Level Sustainability Disclosures: The Strategy of Small Steps

The Sustainable Finance Disclosure Regulation is systematically structured in such a way as to allow demonstrating to the potential investor the varying levels of financial product's – and partly also service's – sustainability-related ambition. Below is an overview of those SFDR product categories, which are sometimes called SFDR-Article-Products:

Art. 6 SFDR products (and advice): Integration of sustainability risks. The first step in approaching the product's sustainability-related ambition topic is through the mechanism of *Art. 6(1) SFDR*, which requires the *financial market participant* to make clear to the potential investor if and how its financial product considers sustainability risks. If these are considered, the financial market participant has to explain how that is done; if not – an explanation as to why not is required to be provided. Products integrating sustainability risks are sometimes called SFDR-Art. 6-products. This term is technically not entirely precise as Art. 6 SFDR also covers and leaves space for products which consider sustainability risks to be not relevant. The European Commission also clarified in its SFDR Q&A of July 2021 that sustainability risk integration does not per se trigger the disclosure requirements of Art. 8 SFDR[21], i.e. does not qualify as "promotion" of "E" and "S" characteristics in the sense of Art. 8 SFDR. Under *Art. 6(2) SFDR*, a comparable regulatory logic as for financial market participants under Art. 6(1) SFDR is applied to *investment advisors* and investment advice. In practice and on the market, though, it is not common to speak of "Art. 6 SFDR investment advice" as that is done with regard to financial products. Note that Art. 7 Taxonomy Regulation sets additional requirements for financial products falling under the scope of Art. 6 SFDR disclosure requirements to include information on Taxonomy-alignment[22].

Art. 7 SFDR products: Consideration of PASI. The provision of Art. 7 SFDR requires the financial market participant to make a disclosure regarding principal adverse sustainability impacts ("PASI") consideration at financial product level. Such disclosure needs to be done in accordance with the requirements of Art. 7 SFDR, which follow and are structured according to the same logic as Art. 6 SFDR on sustainability risk integration. The rule of Art. 7 SFDR is structured in a way which establishes a connection of that rule with the requirement of Art. 4 SFDR, which deals with PASI consideration at entity level. The provision of Art. 7 SFDR is formulated in a way which may be interpreted as leading to a conclusion that only products manufactured by entities which consider PASI at entity level according to Art. 4 SFDR can claim they consider PASI at product level in accordance to Art. 7 SFDR. While interpretative discussion on that may continue for some time, the European Commission clarified in its SFDR Q&A of May 2022 that Art. 7 SFDR does not imply such limitation, meaning that products considering PASI in the sense of Art. 7 SFDR can be manufactured also by entities which do not consider PASI at the entity level in accordance to Art. 4

---

[21] SFDR Q&A 7/2021, p. 8.
[22] For further details, see Section IV.3.

SFDR.[23] As it was the last SFDR provision to come into force, it was somewhat below the radar until quite recently. It certainly bears substantial potential and room for interpretative debate, particularly in context of its interplay with the third sustainability preference under MiFID II (PASI consideration at financial instrument level).

Art. 8 SFDR products: Promotion of "E" or "S" characteristics. This product category is dedicated to financial products that "promote" the environmental and social characteristics. What exactly is meant by "promotion" has been officially clarified by the European Commission only after SFDR's go-live date, in its SFDR Q&A of July 2021.[24] For SFDR's purposes, the term "promotion" is to be understood in a technical, broad manner and the quoted European Commission's Q&A document provides good overview what the category entails (for the relevant Q&A wording excerpt, see information box below).[25]

Regarding the general characteristics of Art. 8 SFDR products, in the words of the European Commission itself, that provision "lays down transparency rules for financial products that have a sustainability-related ambition lower than the ambition of financial products subject to Art. 9".[26] While there is quite some debate ongoing on what exactly the Art. 8 SFDR shall entail, it can certainly be said that as such it does not qualify to make the product automatically eligible for one of the three MiFID II preferences, i.e. is not a "sustainable investment" for that purpose.

The provision of Art. 8 SFDR is to be treated with particular care also in context of the above outlined debate on the topic that SFDR is not a labelling regime. ESMA's chair Verena Ross reemphasized and once more clarified that point in her May 2022 speech noting that SFDR is not labelling regime and that SFDR article products are not "quality labels" for sustainability, adding that the authority is particularly concerned with regard to how Art. 8 products are positioned vis-à-vis the investor.[27]

Conceptually, Art. 8 SFDR may perhaps be best understood as a *"catch all ESG"-provision*, with an intention to cover the entire range of sustainability related claims, starting from the most basic indication or sign of such ambition, and ending with products which include substantial amount of assets flowing into sustainable activities as defined in Art. 2(17) SFDR and Art. 2(1) Taxonomy Regulation. The amount of "sustainable investments" under Art. 8

---

[23] SFDR Q&A 5/2022, p. 1.
[24] SFDR Q&A 7/2021, p. 8.
[25] SFDR Q&A 7/2021, p. 8.
[26] SFDR Q&A 7/2021, p. 7.
[27] *Ross*.

SFDR can range from 0% to 100%. To the extent SFDR is seen as an antigreenwashing regime, it is the Art. 8 SFDR which should be the primary provision for fulfilling that purpose by setting the barrier very low for triggering SFDR's disclosure duties as soon as one "promotes" sustainability characteristics and thus "catch" all the sustainability/ESG "talkers" into the regulation's disclosure framework. The mandated disclosures as tools of that framework then show to the investor, first, what the financial product manufacturer's product-related "talk" exactly means, and second, whether the product indeed "walks" that "talk". That there is no threshold set by the legislator for Art. 8 SFDR products is in line with the legislator's intention – to catch all sustainability-related claims, to capture even the most modest sustainability-related element of the product.[28]

Content-wise, also for purposes of MiFID II client sustainability preferences, a financial instrument/product is only eligible for recommendation as fulfilling such client's sustainability preferences if it includes a minimum proportion in Art. 2(17) SFDR, Art. 2(1) Taxonomy Regulation investments or instruments/products considering PASI, as per investor's individual selection. It its SFDR Q&A 7/2021, the European Commission emphasizes that "where a product has an environmental objective and does not meet the do not significant harm as referred to in Article 2(17) of Regulation (EU) 2019/2088, qualifies as Article 8 product."[29]

The European Commission's SFDR Q&A 7/2021 document provides further useful clarification with regard to the design of the products, by emphasizing that "Article 8 of Regulation (EU) 2019/2088 remains neutral in terms of design of financial products. It does not prescribe certain elements such as the composition of investments or minimum investment thresholds, the eligible investment targets, and neither does it determine eligible investing styles, investment tools, strategies or methodologies to be employed." Due to this neutrality and openness of Art. 8 SFDR product category, there is nothing in the requirements of Art. 8 that would prevent to continue "applying various current market practises, tools and strategies and a combination thereof such as *screening, exclusion strategies, best-in-class/universe, thematic investing, certain redistribution of profits or fees.*"[30] This could include approaches aiming at reduction of negative externalities caused by the underlying investments, which would at least in part include Art. 7 SFDR products considering PASI.[31] Positioning a financial product by "promoting", e.g. in the investment policy, the sustainability-related aspect that the product is complying with certain en-

---

[28] For ESMA's view on that last aspect, see *Ross*.
[29] SFDR Q&A 7/2021, p. 7.
[30] SFDR Q&A 7/2021, p. 8. Emphasis added.
[31] SFDR Q&A 7/2021, p. 8.

vironmental, social or sustainability requirements or restrictions laid down by law, including international conventions, or voluntary codes would make such product subject Article 8 disclosure regime. The first "filter" through which Art. 8 SFDR mechanism brings a sustainability-related claim is asking to put it into a form of a pre-contractual disclosure, with an added requirement that those disclosures "must refer" to those environmental or social elements which are "binding during the whole holding period" and "which are used for the description of the extent to which environmental or social characteristics are met."[32]

Art. 8 SFDR and the term "promotion" plays a key role under SFDR's framework, particularly in that framework's purpose to prevent greenwashing, make the life of potential green washers as difficult as possible.[33] Activation of that term triggers the application of the extensive and systematic SFDR disclosure regime. What qualifies as "promotion" under SFDR is therefore of essential importance for properly understanding and applying Art. 8 as a key element in SFDR's system. European Commission's SFDR Q&A of July 2021 explains what "promotion" means, making clear how broad and far-reaching the concept is:

> **"Promotion" of E/S characteristics – SFDR's concept**[34]
>
> "The term 'promotion' within the meaning of Article 8 of Regulation (EU) 2019/2088 encompasses, by way of example, *direct or indirect claims*, information, reporting, disclosures as well as an *impression* that investments pursued by the given financial product also consider environmental or social characteristics in terms of investment policies, goals, targets or objectives or a general ambition in, but not limited to, pre-contractual and periodic documents or marketing communications, advertisements, product *categorisation*, description of investment strategies or asset allocation, information on the *adherence to sustainability-related financial product standards and labels, use of product names or designations*, memoranda or issuing documents, factsheets, specifications about conditions for automatic enrolment or compliance with sectoral exclusions or statutory requirements regardless of the form used, such as on paper, durable media, by means of websites, or electronic data rooms." (emphasis added)

Note that Art. 6 Taxonomy Regulation expands the scope of Art. 8 SFDR disclosure requirements to include information on Taxonomy-alignment.[35]

Art. 9 SFDR products: Sustainable investments as an objective. The Art. 9 SFDR product-level disclosure regime is designed for financial products which have sustainable investments as their objective. It is a disclosure re-

---

[32] SFDR Q&A 7/2021, p. 8.
[33] *Zukas/Trafkowski*, p. 20.
[34] SFDR Q&A 7/2021, p. 8.
[35] For further details, see Section IV.3.

7. Financial Product Level Sustainability Disclosures

gime for products with highest level of sustainability ambition. As the European Commission's SFDR Q&A 7/2021 puts it, "where such financial products do not have 'sustainable investment' as their objective, as referred to in Article 9, they are considered to fall under Article 8."[36] Emphasis of Art. 8 and 9 SFDR disclosure regime's interplay with MiFID II sustainability preferences is important to keep in mind: the different SFDR product sustainability ambition of Art. 8 compared to Art. 9 SFDR is "key to determine the access of end investors to financial products that are ambitious enough to meet their sustainability preferences."[37]

In contrast to Art. 8 SFDR products, Art. 9 SFDR products shall generally only invest in underlying assets which qualify as "sustainable investments" in the sense of Art. 2(17) SFDR.[38] Exceptions can be made from that general principle: "A financial product, in order to meet requirements in accordance with prudential, product-related sector specific rules may next to 'sustainable investments', also include investments for certain specific purposes such as hedging or liquidity", under the condition that these, in order to fit the overall financial product's sustainable investments' objective, have to meet minimum environmental or social safeguards."[39]

According to Recital 19 Taxonomy Regulation, the term "sustainable investments" under Art. 2(17) SFDR includes "environmentally sustainable investments" under Art. 2(1) Taxonomy Regulation, under the condition that those meet the DNSH test under SFDR. The ESAs' position on this additional DNSH test has changed in the course of L2 RTS preparatory works[40] (for the relevant document excerpt, see information box below).

Similar to Art. 8 SFDR, Art. 9 SFDR "remains neutral in terms of the product design, or investing styles, investment tools, strategies or methodologies to be employed or other elements", but the "product documentation must include information how the given mix complies with the 'sustainable investment' objective of the financial product in order to comply with the 'no significant harm principle'" of Art. 2(17) SFDR.[41] "Impact investing" understood as the form of sustainable finance with highest ambition is often given as an example of Art. 9 SFDR product category, thought it has to be kept in mind that not the products name, but whether it fulfils the requirements of Art. 9 SFDR is decisive for purposes of such qualification.

---

[36] SFDR Q&A 7/2021, p. 5.
[37] SFDR Q&A 7/2021, p. 5.
[38] SFDR Q&A 7/2021, p. 5.
[39] SFDR Q&A 7/2021, p. 5.
[40] SFDR/TR L2 RTS draft final report 10/2021, p. 8.
[41] SFDR Q&A 7/2021, p. 5.

European Commission's SFDR Q&A 7/2021 gives a good overview of what the product category falling under Art. 9 SFDR disclosure regime entails and how it should be differentiated from Art. 8 SFDR products. It needs to be noted that – similar as Art. 8 SFDR products – also Art. 9 SFDR products as such do not figure as one of three sustainability preferences under new MiFID II rules. This means that also Art. 9 SFDR products are only of direct relevance as a product eligible for recommendation for clients with sustainability preferences if and to the extent it includes Art. 2(17) SFDR, Art. 2(1) Taxonomy Regulation investments or consider PASI. It needs to be noted that Art. 9 SFDR disclosure regime is more extensive compared to Art. 8 SFDR disclosure regime allowing the client to check even more thoroughly what he or she gets as compared to what the product claims to be in terms of sustainability-consideration. Note that Art. 5 Taxonomy Regulation expands the scope of Art. 9 SFDR disclosure requirements to include information on Taxonomy-alignment.[42]

"Do No Significant Harm"-Principle: SFDR vs. TR standard – ESAs' changed view 10/2021[43]
"For one of the aspects of the RTS, the ESAs changed their approach in the final report compared to the Consultation Paper. In the Consultation Paper the ESAs had proposed to derogate from the general SFDR RTS relating to the principle of Do No Significant Harm (DNSH) (which require taking into account the adverse impact indicators of Annex I of the RTS) for taxonomy-aligned sustainable investments, which already require the detailed DNSH rules of the TR Technical Screening Criteria. However, *as a result of a legal analysis the ESAs concluded that it is not possible to derogate from the general SFDR DNSH RTS for sustainable investments that are taxonomy-aligned, that derogation has been removed.* As a result, the *DNSH related rules will be applied to all sustainable investments including the taxonomy-aligned investments.* While the ESAs regret this, as they believe this will adversely affect taxonomy-aligned investments, this means that the ESAs' proposal for publication of a statement on taxonomy-alignment, as included in the Consultation Paper, no longer serves any purpose and has therefore been removed from the final report." (*emphasis added*)

b) General Remarks on SFDR-Article-Product Categories

The SFDR-article-product categories are sometimes described as "different shades of green" which is an informal term to show their different levels of sustainability-related ambition. First, by referring to just "green" it is obviously also not covering the entire spectrum of potential sustainability-related

---

[42] For further details, see Section IV.3.
[43] SFDR/TR L2 RTS draft final report 10/2021, p. 8.

ambition SFDR disclosure regime is able to cover. Art. 8 and Art. 9 SFDR are also sometimes referred to as "light green" and "dark green", even in official EU documents[44]. These are also rather informal terms, with similar limitations as the "shades of green". Second, they should be avoided in today's context due to an additional potential irritation especially with regard to Art. 8 SFDR products implying that "light green" refers to some kind of threshold for "green" content in those products or even sustainability "quality label", while SFDR is not a labelling regime and in fact there may be none of that "green" in the product, especially in a case of Art. 8 SFDR products.[45] Though such colourful informal descriptions may be useful to

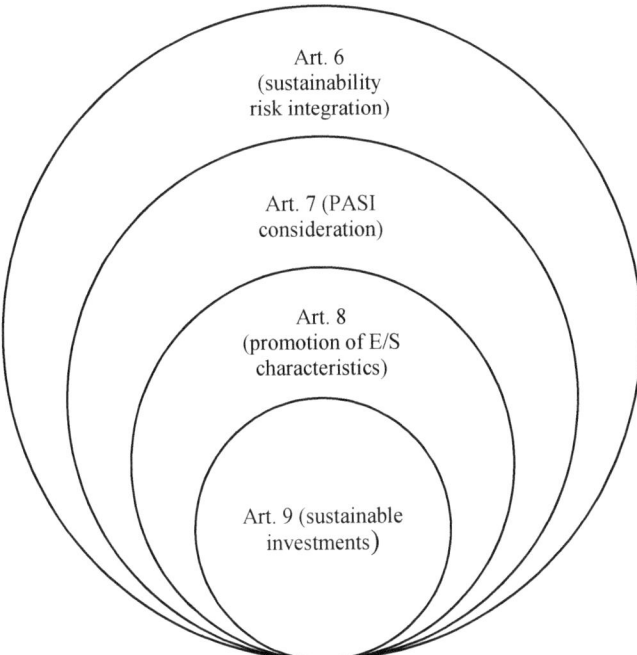

Legend: "PASI" = principal adverse sustainability impacts.

Note that only Art. 9 SFDR products shall, as a matter of principle, consist of sustainable investments in the sense of Art. 2(17) SFDR only. Art. 8 SFDR may include sustainable investments, but may also not include them (no threshold, "catch all"-provision) and is therefore to be seen as a value-neutral provision, which – due to its open character – plays key role in the SFDR's purpose as anti-greenwashing regime.

Figure: Overview SFDR-article-product disclosure categories – Varying degrees of sustainability-related ambition

---

[44] SFDR RTS final draft report 2/2021, p. 5.
[45] See Section III.3. for more details.

show the general difference in terms of sustainability-related ambition between Art. 8 and Art. 9 SFDR products which indeed conceptually exists, they should be avoided as they create an impression of a sustainability quality labels and thus pose a greenwashing risk.

SFDR-Art.	Art.-Title	Requirement	Transparency channel
Art. 6(1) *"Comply ..."*	Transparency of the integration of sustainability risks	– manner of integrating sustainability risks in investment decisions and – impact of sustainability risks on their products' returns ➜ Applicable to financial market participants	Pre-contractual disclosure
Art. 6(1) *... or explain"*	Transparency of the integration of sustainability risks	– if considered not relevant-reasons therefor ("Comply or explain") ➜ Applicable to financial market participants	Pre-contractual disclosure
Art. 7(1) *"Comply ..."*	Transparency of adverse sustainability impacts at financial product level	– a clear and reasoned explanation of *whether*, and, if so, *how* a financial product considers principal adverse impacts on sustainability factors; – statement that information on principal adverse impacts on sustainability factors is available in the information to be disclosed pursuant to Article 11(2) SFDR ➜ Applicable to financial market participants which have made use of the option under Art. 4(1)(a) SFDR, i.e. consider PASI at entity level	Pre-contractual disclosure

(continue next page)

7. Financial Product Level Sustainability Disclosures

(overview continued)

SFDR-Art.	Art.-Title	Requirement	Transparency channel
Art. 7(2) "... or explain"	Transparency of adverse sustainability impacts at financial product level	– for each financial product, include a statement that the financial market participant (1) does not consider the adverse impacts of investment decisions on sustainability factors and (2) the reasons therefor ➜ Applicable to financial market participants which are eligible for and have made use of the option under Art. 4(1)(b) SFDR, i.e. do not consider PASI at entity level Note that SFDR Q&A 5/2022 clarified that financial market participant allowed to opt-out from Art. 4 SFDR PASI consideration regime *"may, notwithstanding the criteria set out in Article 7(1), first subparagraph, of Regulation (EU) 2019/2088, manufacture a financial product that pursues a reduction of negative externalities caused by the investments underlying that product."*[46]	Pre-contractual disclosure
Art. 8	Transparency of the promotion of environmental or social characteristics in pre-contractual disclosures	– information on *how* those characteristics are met – if an index has been designated as a reference benchmark, information on whether and how this index is consistent with those characteristics. ➜ Applicable to financial market participants	Pre-contractual disclosure
Art. 9	Transparency of sustainable investments in pre-contractual disclosures	– explanation on *how* that objective is to be attained – specific requirements for cases where an index has been designated as a reference benchmark – specific requirements for products having reduction of carbon emissions as an objective	Pre-contractual disclosure

---

[46] SFDR Q&A 5/2022, p. 1. Emphasis added.

SFDR-Art.	Art.-Title	Requirement	Transparency channel
Art. 10 (for Art. 8 and 9 products)	Transparency of the promotion of environmental or social characteristics and of sustainable investments on websites	– a description of the environmental or social characteristics or the sustainable investment objective; – information on the methodologies used to assess, measure and monitor the environmental or social characteristics or the impact of the sustainable investments selected for the financial product, including its data sources, screening criteria for the underlying assets and the relevant sustainability indicators used to measure the environmental or social characteristics or the overall sustainable impact of the financial product; – the information referred to in Articles 8 and 9; – the information referred to in Article 11. ➜ Applicable to financial market participants, Art. 8 and 9 products	Website
Art. 11 (for Art. 8 and 9 products)	Transparency of the promotion of environmental or social characteristics and of sustainable investments in periodic reports	For Art. 8 products: – the extent to which environmental or social characteristics are met For Art. 9 products: – the overall sustainability-related impact of the financial product by means of relevant sustainability indicators; or – where an index has been designated as a reference benchmark, a comparison between the overall sustainability-related impact of the financial product with the impacts of the designated index and of a broad market index through sustainability indicators.	Periodic reports

Overview: Financial product level disclosure requirements under SFDR

In this context, it needs to be reminded that the Taxonomy Regulation includes changes to the original SFDR version and adds an additional, Taxonomy-alignment related disclosure layer to Art. 6, 8 and 9 SFDR disclosures, with substantial level of additional technical detail.[47]

Referring to the point on SFDR as not labelling regime discussed in detail in Section III.3., it is important to keep in mind that for purposes of assessing a financial product's sustainability-related quality not the SFDR-article-6/8/9-categories shall be utilized, but the substance/materiality-focused provisions defining what qualifies as "sustainable investment" (Art. 2(17) SFDR), "environmentally sustainable investment" (Art. 2(1) Taxonomy Regulation) as well as the legislative ratio behind the SFDR provisions on PASI consideration on entity and product level (Art. 4 and Art. 7 SFDR).

8. Marketing Communications

We explained in Section III.3. that the Sustainable Finance Disclosure Regulation is not a labelling regime, but a transparency and anti-greenwashing regime. Though marketing communications understood as talking about what a company or a product does (or claims to do) is the organisation's primary touchpoint with the outside world and thus of essential importance for reaching legislator's purpose of preventing greenwashing, this entire area is regulated by SFDR with a rather simple, general rule. That rule is stated in Art. 13 SFDR, titled "Marketing communications". It is addressed to both financial market participants and financial advisers and requires them to "ensure that their marketing communications *do not contradict* the information disclosed pursuant to this Regulation." In other words, saying one thing about the firm's, its services, and especially financial products sustainability-related characteristics in SFDR disclosures on the firm's website, in pre-contractual documents, periodic reporting and different thing in marketing communications may not only bring problems in the relationship with an investor, cause problems under relevant applicable/governing law, but would also mean a regulatory breach in the sense of SFDR. It needs to be kept in mind that this no-contradiction-requirement has potential to cover only part of greenwashing related risks, also because a contradiction between the disclosures made via various disclosure channels will not always mean the firm is "overselling" its green credentials or pretending to be more sustainable that it is actually the case (i.e. committing greenwashing).

---

[47] For more information on this aspect, see Section IV.3.

IV. Europe's "Green Vocabulary": The Taxonomy Regulation

Taxonomy Regulation is an action item number 1 in the EU's Sustainable Finance Action Plan. It describes itself as *"the most important and urgent action envisaged by the action plan"* (Recital 6 TR). That ambition is to set a legal standard on what qualifies as "environmentally sustainable investment" (sometimes also called "green investment" or, even more technically, "Taxonomy-aligned investment").

1. "Let's Get Technical"

In essence, the Taxonomy Regulation does one thing which makes it so fundamental for the world of sustainable finance: It defines what qualifies as an "environmentally sustainable" investment. In the words of the Taxonomy Regulation itself, *"[t]his Regulation establishes the criteria for determining whether an economic activity qualifies as environmentally sustainable for the purposes of establishing the degree to which an investment is environmentally sustainable"* (Art. 1(1)). *What* it does is not less important as compare to *how* it does it: namely, with a highly detailed level of technicality, to which we will return when discussing that definition in more detail.

As for the Taxonomy Regulation's scope, Art. 1(2) TR aims to have it applied to the following areas:

- *measures adopted by Member States or by the Union* that set out requirements for financial market participants or issuers in respect of *financial products or corporate bonds* that are made available as environmentally sustainable;
- *financial market participants* that make available financial products;
- *undertakings which are subject to the obligation to publish a non-financial statement* or a consolidated non-financial statement pursuant to Article 19a or Article 29a of Directive 2013/34/EU (i.e. NFRD) of the European Parliament and of the Council, respectively.

While the first part of the rule makes clear the Taxonomy Regulation's function as a green glossary for both Member States and the Union itself, it also ads an important clarification that the Regulation's scope is not limited to financial products as the term is defined under SFDR and Taxonomy Regulation. The Taxonomy's standard shall also apply to corporate bonds which are made available as "environmentally sustainable" (the so-called "green bonds"). The second part of the rule, addressed to financial market participants "that make available financial instruments", refers to additional disclosures the Taxonomy Regulation prescribes for SFDR products, a disclosure requirement with a very substantial impact, which we discuss in more detail in Section IV.3. Finally, the third part is about the so-called "non-financial" corporate reporting (better: corporate sustainability reporting)[1], which the Taxonomy extends with an obligation to report Taxonomy alignment.

2. Defining "Environmentally Sustainable Investment"

The Taxonomy Regulation defines the term "environmentally sustainable investment" in its Art. 2(1). It is a simple definition as the only thing it actually says is that environmentally sustainable investment is an *"investment in one or several economic activities that qualify as environmentally sustainable under this Regulation"*. Accordingly, the concept of "environmentally sustainable activity" is a key concept for defining what environmentally sustainable investment is. The concept of environmentally sustainable activity is defined in Art. 3 Taxonomy Regulation, which not only describes the key elements an economic activity needs to fulfil in order to qualify as environmentally sustainable, but also provides extensive, technical guidance on how those elements need to be understood. This is done by cross-referring to other provisions of the Taxonomy Regulation, which describe in detail what each of those elements consists of.

---

[1] For the reasons why this term shall be preferred in modern sustainable finance context, see Section VI.4.

"Environmentally sustainable investment" – Taxonomy Regulation's definition
Article 2. Definitions (1) 'environmentally sustainable investment' means an *investment in* one or several *economic activities that qualify as environmentally sustainable under* this Regulation; …"
Article 3. Criteria for environmentally sustainable economic activities For the purposes of establishing the degree to which an investment is environmentally sustainable, an economic activity shall qualify as environmentally sustainable where that economic activity: (a) *contributes substantially* to one or more of the **environmental objectives** set out in Article 9 in accordance with Articles 10 to 16; (b) **does not significantly harm** *any of the environmental* objectives set out in Article 9 in accordance with Article 17; (c) is carried out in compliance with the **minimum safeguards** laid down in Article 18; and (d) complies with **technical screening criteria** that have been established by the Commission in accordance with Article 10(3), 11(3), 12(2), 13(2), 14(2) or 15(2)." (emphasis added)

Legend: "E" refers to "environmental objectives", a list of objectives as per Art. 9 Taxonomy Regulation. "DNSH" = "Do Not Significant Harm"-principle.

Figure: Definition of "environmentally sustainable investment" – core elements

Taxonomy Regulation's disclosure obligations for these environmental objectives come into application gradually, starting from 1 January 2022 and, as a second step, continuing from 1 January 2023, that line of order certainly also serving as a signal as to their prioritization. What qualifies as "substantial contribution" to those is prescribed in detailed fashion in Articles 10 to 16 Taxonomy Regulation, while Art. 17 explains in detail what the "Do not significant harm"-principle means for purposes of the Taxonomy Regulation. Additionally and very importantly, Art. 16 Taxonomy Regulation includes a provision on the so-called "enabling activities", which qualify as "substantially contributing" to one or more environmental objectives set out in Art. 9 Taxonomy Regulation. Taxonomy Regulation's delegated acts provide further

2. Defining "Environmentally Sustainable Investment"

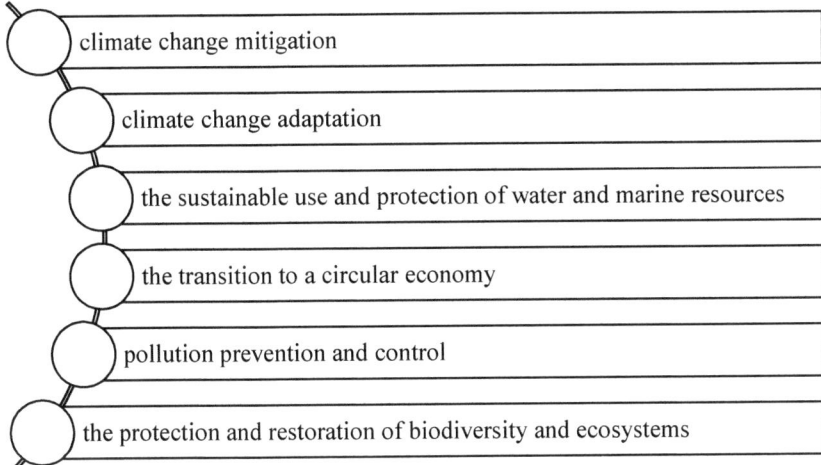

Figure: List of "Environmental objectives" – Taxonomy Regulation

details regarding which technical criteria an economic activity needs to fulfill in order to qualify as an environmentally sustainable.

As for the priorities and actions requiring most urgency, the Action Plan states clearly "E" (environmental considerations) should be prioritized, with topics of climate change mitigation and adaptation coming first and the rest to follow afterwards: "While the *taxonomy work will begin on climate change mitigation*, the scope will be progressively expanded to climate change adaptation and other environmental issues and, later on, to social sustainability. Such an *approach reflects the urgency to act against climate change* and to meet our long-term climate and energy targets."[2]

In order to qualify as environmentally sustainable, an economic activity shall not only substantially contribute to one of the environmental objectives as per Art. 9 SFDR and do not significantly harm the other environmental objectives as per Art. 17 of the Taxonomy Regulation. It has also to fulfil the so called "Minimum safeguards"-test as per Art. 18 Taxonomy Regulation. That test is summarized under the below figure.

---

[2] Sustainable Finance Action Plan, pp. 11–12. Emphasis added.

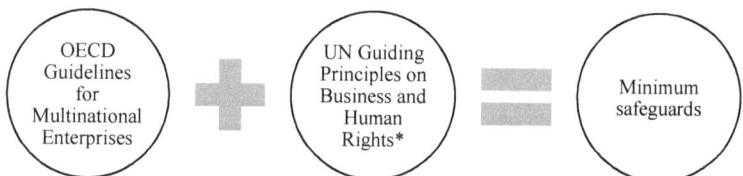

* Includes the principles and rights set out in the eight fundamental conventions identified in the Declaration of the International Labour Organisation on Fundamental Principles and Rights at Work and the International Bill of Human Rights.

Figure: "Minimum safeguards"-test[3] – Taxonomy Regulation

3. TR/SFDR Interplay

As the full title of the Taxonomy Regulation itself makes clear, beside defining what constitutes an environmentally sustainable activity and investment, what the Taxonomy Regulation does is introducing changes to the SFDR[4]. Those changes to the SFDR require to add further layer of Taxonomy-alignment related information to the SFDR's Article 6, 8 and 9 disclosures. The Taxonomy does that by means of Articles 5, 6 and 7 Taxonomy Regulation, which, accordingly, set requirements for providing that additional level of Taxonomy-alignment related information for the SFDR's Article 9, 8 and 6 disclosure regimes.

---

[3] OECD Guidelines for Multinational Enterprises, 2011; UN Guiding Principles on Business and Human Rights (UNGPs), endorsed by the United Nations Human Rights Council on June 16, 2011.

[4] Regulation (EU) 2020/852 of the European Parliament and of the Council of 18 June 2020 on the establishment of a framework to facilitate sustainable investment, and amending Regulation (EU) 2019/2088, OJ L 198 pp. 13–43. Emphasis added.

3. TR/SFDR Interplay

SFDR product disclosure category	Additional Taxonomy-alignment disclosure layer	Disclosure channel	Additional Taxonomy-alignment disclosure layer content
Art. 9 SFDR	Art. 5 TR	Pre-contractual and periodic	**Article 5. Transparency of** *environmentally sustainable investments* **in pre-contractual disclosures and in periodic reports** Where a financial product as referred to in Article 9(1), (2) or (3) of Regulation (EU) 2019/2088 *invests in an economic activity that contributes to an environmental objective within the meaning of point (17) of Article 2 of that Regulation*, the information to be disclosed in accordance with Articles 6(3) and 11(2) of that Regulation shall include the following: (a) the information *on the environmental objective or environmental objectives set out in Article 9* of this Regulation to which the investment underlying the financial product contributes; and (b) a description of *how and to what extent the investments underlying the financial product are in economic activities that qualify as environmentally sustainable under Article 3* of this Regulation. The description referred to in point (b) of the first subparagraph of this Article shall specify the *proportion* of investments in environmentally sustainable economic activities selected for the financial product, including details on the proportions of enabling and transitional activities referred to in Article 16 and Article 10(2), respectively, as a percentage of all investments selected for the financial product. *(emphasis added)*

SFDR product disclosure category	Additional Taxonomy-alignment disclosure layer	Disclosure channel	Additional Taxonomy-alignment disclosure layer content
Art. 8 SFDR	Art. 6 TR	Pre-contractual and periodic	**Article 6. Transparency of financial products that** *promote environmental characteristics* **in pre-contractual disclosures and in periodic reports** Where a financial product as referred to in Article 8(1) of Regulation (EU) 2019/2088 promotes environmental characteristics, Article 5 of this Regulation shall apply *mutatis mutandis*. The information to be disclosed in accordance with Articles 6(3) and 11(2) of Regulation (EU) 2019/2088 shall be *accompanied by the following statement*: (*emphasis added*) 'The "do no significant harm" principle applies only to those investments underlying the financial product that take into account the EU criteria for environmentally sustainable economic activities. The investments underlying the remaining portion of this financial product do not take into account the EU criteria for environmentally sustainable economic activities.'
Art. 6 SFDR (not subject to Art. 8/9 SFDR)	Art. 7 TR	Pre-contractual and periodic	**Article 7. Transparency of other financial products in pre-contractual disclosures and in periodic reports** Where a financial product is *not subject to* Article 8(1) or to Article 9(1), (2) or (3) of Regulation (EU) 2019/2088, the information to be disclosed in accordance with the provisions of sectoral legislation referred to in Articles 6(3) and 11(2) of that Regulation shall be *accompanied by the following statement*: (*emphasis added*) 'The investments underlying this financial product do not take into account the EU criteria for environmentally sustainable economic activities.'

Overview: TR / SFDR interplay – product level disclosures

Note that Art. 27 Taxonomy Regulation on entry into force and application of the Taxonomy Regulation makes clear that the Regulation's disclosure obligations with regard to the environmental objectives set out in Art. 9 Taxonomy Regulation shall come into application gradually, starting with the environmental objectives of climate change mitigation and climate change adaptation set out in Art. 9(a)–(b) first, per 1 January 2022, following by the environmental objectives set out in Art. 9(c)–(f) per 1 January 2023 (sustainable use and protection of water and marine resources; transition to a circular economy; pollution prevention and control; protection and restoration of biodiversity and ecosystems).

As for the scope of Taxonomy-alignment reporting obligations as per Art. 6 TR, SFDR Q&A 5/2022 adds an important clarification that for triggering the application of Art. 6 Taxonomy Regulation, "it is irrelevant if a financial product commits to invest in economic activities that contribute to an environmental objective within the meaning of Article 2, point (17), of Regulation (EU) 2019/2088."[5] It further clarifies that "a financial product referred to in Article 8(1) of Regulation (EU) 2019/2088 that promotes environmental characteristics must include in the pre-contractual disclosures, based on an assessment of reliable data with regard to whether investments will be in economic activities that contribute to an environmental objective, information according to Article 6 of Regulation (EU) 2020/852 if that is the case." The conceptual implications of this clarification are yet to be fully understood, so are the implications of the European Commission's clarifications in the immediately following paragraph of the same Q&A document regarding reflection of changes of financial product's investments over time in pre-contractual documentation[6].

4. TR/NFRD Interplay

Following a similar logic as for SFDR's product disclosures, the Taxonomy Regulation's Art. 8 adds a requirement to disclose an additional layer of information at entity level for the companies subject to the Non-Financial Reporting Directive's corporate reporting regime. While its current reach is limited to large companies subject to NFRD reporting obligations, this requirement may be seen as first step in the effort to feed the market with sustainability-related data reported by the companies directly.

---

[5] SFDR Q&A 5/2022, p. 11.
[6] SFDR Q&A 5/2022, p. 11.

NFRD provisions	Additional Taxonomy-alignment disclosure layer	Disclosure channel	Additional Taxonomy-alignment disclosure layer content
Article 19a or Article 29a NFRD	Art. 8 TR	non-financial statement or consolidated non-financial statement	**Article 8. Transparency of undertakings in non-financial statements** 1. Any undertaking which is subject to an obligation to publish non-financial information pursuant to Article 19a or Article 29a of Directive 2013/34/EU shall include in its non-financial statement or consolidated non-financial statement *information on how and to what extent the undertaking's activities are associated with economic activities that qualify as environmentally sustainable under Articles 3 and 9* of this Regulation. 2. In particular, non-financial undertakings shall disclose the following: (a) the *proportion of their turnover* derived from products or services associated with economic activities that qualify as environmentally sustainable under Articles 3 and 9; and (b) *the proportion of their capital expenditure and the proportion of their operating expenditure* related to assets or processes associated with economic activities that qualify as environmentally sustainable under Articles 3 and 9. (*emphasis added*)

Overview: TR / NFRD interplay – entity level disclosures

Art. 8(4) Taxonomy Regulation foresees that the European Commission "shall adopt a delegated act in accordance with Article 23 to supplement paragraphs 1 and 2 of this Article to specify the content and presentation of the information to be disclosed pursuant to those paragraphs, including the methodology to be used in order to comply with them, taking into account the specificities of both financial and non-financial undertakings and the technical screening criteria established pursuant to this Regulation." Such

4. TR/NFRD Interplay

delegated act has been adopted and published in the Official Journal of the EU on 10 December 2021[7]. It supplements Art. 8 Taxonomy Regulation and specifies the content and presentation of information to be disclosed by undertakings subject to Art. 19a and Art. 29a NFRD concerning environmentally sustainable activities and specifying the methodology to comply with that disclosure obligation. Furthermore, it is worth noting that the NFRD has been substantially reshaped as part of the Sustainable Finance Action Plan's "fitness check" (for further details, see Section VI.).

---

[7] Art. 8 TR disclosure delegated act European Commission, Commission Delegated Regulation (EU) 2021/2178 of 6 July 2021 supplementing Regulation (EU) 2020/852 of the European Parliament and of the Council by specifying the content and presentation of information to be disclosed by undertakings subject to Articles 19a or 29a of Directive 2013/34/EU concerning environmentally sustainable economic activities, and specifying the methodology to comply with that disclosure obligation, OJ L 443, pp. 9–67.

V. Centrality of Client's Choice: MiFID II and the New Duty to Inquire on Client's Sustainability Preferences

Falling under the Sustainable Finance Action Plan's Action category number 1 ("Reorienting capital flows towards sustainable investment"), action item number 4 ("Incorporating sustainability when providing financial advice"), changes to MiFID II delegated regulation 2017/565 ("MiFID II delegated act")[1] on investor's sustainability preferences form an essential legislative change under the new European sustainable finance regulatory architecture.

The changes on client's sustainability preferences introduced by the updated MiFID II delegated act are centered around adding a regulatory requirement of asking the client about its sustainability preferences in general and then inquiring into the specifics of those along three categories of financial instruments which are eligible for clients with sustainability preferences under the MiFID II regime. The new requirement is introduced not only to *"raise sustainable finance"*, but also in order for clear signals to be sent to investors regarding their investments so that they can *"avoid stranded assets"* (Recital 2 MiFID II delegated act).

The updated MiFID II delegated act integrates client's sustainability preferences *"as a top up to the suitability assessment"*[2]. Under the MiFID II regulatory framework known before these changes were introduced, firms providing investment advice and portfolio management were required to obtain information on client's *investment objectives (including risk tolerance), ability to bear losses* as well as client's *knowledge and experience*, which was considered to be necessary in order to be able to provide the client products and services that are suitable to him/her as per Art. 54 MiFID II delegated act ("suitability assessment")[3].

---

[1] Commission Delegated Regulation (EU) 2021/1253 of 21 April 2021 amending Delegated Regulation (EU) 2017/565 as regards the integration of sustainability factors, risks and preferences into certain organisational requirements and operating conditions for investment firms, OJ L 277, pp. 1–5.

[2] Explanatory Memorandum to MiFID II delegated act's draft of 21 April 2021, p. 1.

[3] Explanatory Memorandum to MiFID II delegated act's draft of 21 April 2021, p. 1.

Under that old regulatory regime, information on client's investment objectives was generally limited to financial objectives and did not include information on the so-called "non-financial" objectives, such as sustainability preferences. Existing suitability assessments would generally not include questions on client's sustainability preferences and majority of client would not raise such preferences themselves[4]. The introduction of the updated MiFID II delegated act has changed this, with question on client's sustainability preferences now being introduced as part of the new requirements. Under the new rules, investment firms providing financial advice and portfolio management now must carry out a "mandatory assessment of sustainability preferences" of a client[5].

Those changes have started to apply as this paper is submitted publication in August 2022 and are located in the newly introduced Art. 2(7) MiFID II delegated act. The new provision defines what is to be understood under client's/potential client's "sustainability preferences". What qualifies as sustainability preference is not a simple "Yes" or "No" with regard to ESG or sustainability in general. The definition of sustainability preference takes direct reference to the three listed categories of financial instruments and requires to ask the client/potential client to voice its *choice* with regard to two aspects: first, *whether* and, second, *if yes, to what extent* one or more of those listed financial instrument groups "shall be integrated into his or her investment". Those three groups of instruments eligible to recommend for clients with sustainability preferences do not take SFDR Articles 6, 8 or 9 as criteria determining instrument's eligibility for recommendation to clients/potential clients. In fact, it was the Legal Memorandum to MiFID II delegated act's draft which stated for the first time in April 2021 that SFDR is not a labelling regime[6], a view which has been in the meantime strengthened and confirmed in various other statements by the EU Commission and ESMA (for an in-depth overview of this development, see Section III.3.). The financial instrument/product related TR and SFDR categories which MiFID II considers relevant for clients with sustainability preferences are the categories of "environmentally sustainable investment" under Art. 2(1) Taxonomy Regulation, "sustainable investment" under Art. 2(17) SFDR and the concept of PASI consideration, with no direct reference to any specific provision, but known as a concept from Art. 4 and Art. 7 SFDR. Additionally, MiFID II speaks of "financial instruments", while SFDR and Taxonomy Regulation are focused

---

[4] Explanatory Memorandum to MiFID II delegated act's draft of 21 April 2021, p. 1.
[5] Explanatory Memorandum to MiFID II delegated act's draft of 21 April 2021, p. 5.
[6] Explanatory Memorandum to MiFID II delegated act's draft of 21 April 2021, p. 2.

on "financial products", both of which are terms with their own, different regulatory definitions. The Explanatory memorandum to MiFID II delegated act's draft clarifies that the term "financial instrument" is used to reflect the circumstance of different product scopes under SFDR, TR and MiFID II and in order to not restrict the sustainability preferences to financial products in the meaning of SFDR and TR[7]. The new MiFID II provisions on sustainability preferences shall allow investment firms to "recommend not only investment funds, but also other relevant financial instruments."[8]

Two of the three categories of financial instruments eligible for recommendation for clients with sustainability preferences under the new MiFID II regulatory regime take the concept of "minimum proportion" to determine if the instrument/product is substantially sufficient to mirror client's sustainability ambition with regard to the concepts of "environmentally sustainable investment" under Art. 2(1) TR and Art. 2(17) SFDR. As for the third category – instruments/products considering PASI – here, the law does not ask the client to provide "minimum proportion", but asks for his/her choice and determination on "qualitative or quantitative elements demonstrating that consideration." In both cases, client/potential client remains in driver's seat and is free to choose his/her sustainability-related ambition.

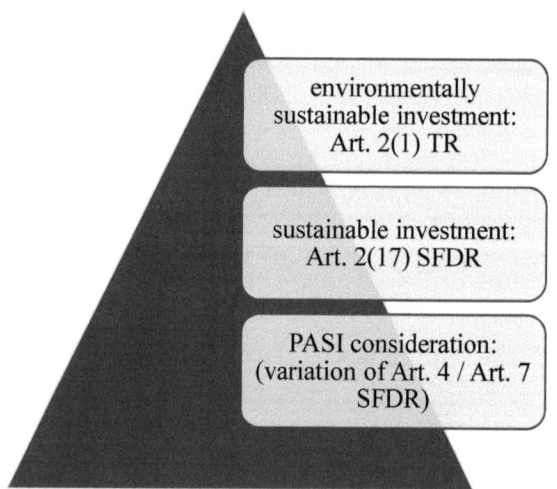

Overview: SFDR/TR concepts –
relevance for sustainability preferences under MiFID II

---

[7] Explanatory Memorandum to MiFID II delegated act's draft of 21 April 2021, p. 5.

[8] Explanatory Memorandum to MiFID II delegated act's draft of 21 April 2021, p. 5.

V. Centrality of Client's Choice

"Sustainability preferences" – MiFID II definition (new)
Art. 2(7) MiFID II delegated regulation

"sustainability preferences" means a client's or potential client's choice as to *whether* and, *if so, to what extent*, one or more of the following *financial instruments* shall be integrated into his or her investment:

(a) a financial instrument for which the client or potential client determines that a *minimum proportion* shall be invested in *environmentally sustainable investments* as defined in Article 2, point (1), of Regulation (EU) 2020/852 of the European Parliament and of the Council;

(b) a financial instrument for which the client or potential client determines that a *minimum proportion* shall be invested in *sustainable investments* as defined in Article 2, point (17), of Regulation (EU) 2019/2088 of the European Parliament and of the Council;

(c) a financial instrument that *considers principal adverse impacts on sustainability factors* where qualitative or quantitative elements demonstrating that consideration are determined by the client or potential client; *(emphasis added)*

"Financial instrument" – MiFID II definition

Art. 4(1)(15) MiFID II

'financial instrument' means those instruments specified in Section C of Annex I;

ANNEX I MiFID II: LISTS OF SERVICES AND ACTIVITIES AND FINANCIAL INSTRUMENTS

SECTION C

Financial instruments

(1) Transferable securities;

(2) Money-market instruments;

(3) Units in collective investment undertakings;

(4) Options, futures, swaps, forward rate agreements and any other derivative contracts relating to securities, currencies, interest rates or yields, emission allowances or other derivatives instruments, financial indices or financial measures which may be settled physically or in cash;

(5) Options, futures, swaps, forwards and any other derivative contracts relating to commodities that must be settled in cash or may be settled in cash at the option of one of the parties other than by reason of default or other termination event;

(6) Options, futures, swaps, and any other derivative contract relating to commodities that can be physically settled provided that they are traded on a regulated market, a MTF, or an OTF, except for wholesale energy products traded on an OTF that must be physically settled;

(7) Options, futures, swaps, forwards and any other derivative contracts relating to commodities, that can be physically settled not otherwise mentioned in point 6 of this Section and not being for commercial purposes, which have the characteristics of other derivative financial instruments;

> (8) Derivative instruments for the transfer of credit risk;
>
> (9) Financial contracts for differences;
>
> (10) Options, futures, swaps, forward rate agreements and any other derivative contracts relating to climatic variables, freight rates or inflation rates or other official economic statistics that must be settled in cash or may be settled in cash at the option of one of the parties other than by reason of default or other termination event, as well as any other derivative contracts relating to assets, rights, obligations, indices and measures not otherwise mentioned in this Section, which have the characteristics of other derivative financial instruments, having regard to whether, inter alia, they are traded on a regulated market, OTF, or an MTF;
>
> (11) Emission allowances consisting of any units recognised for compliance with the requirements of Directive 2003/87/EC (Emissions Trading Scheme).

As a consequence of the above-described conceptual change in understanding that SFDR-article-products are neither labels, nor do they play a central role in determining a financial product's eligibility for recommendation to clients with sustainability preferences under the new MiFID II regime, the following overview might be helpful in contextualising the role of SFDR-article-products in the new European sustainable finance regulatory architecture and especially their interplay with the concept of "sustainable investment" under Art. 2(17) SFDR.

> **Overview – Interplay: SFDR-article-products vs. "sustainable investment"**
>
> **Art. 6 SFDR products** (integrating/not integrating sustainability risks): Art. 6 products *integrating* sustainability risks, as such, do not qualify as "sustainable investments" and this product category per se does in essence not say anything about the amount of "sustainable investment" in the product, i.e. is neutral in that regard. Statement that a product integrates sustainability risks per se does not trigger the application of Art. 8 disclosure regime[9]. An Art. 6 SFDR product stating it does *not integrate* sustainability risks can still trigger Art. 8 SFDR disclosure regime if it includes statements which qualify as "promotion" of environmental or social characteristics (as counter-intuitive as it may sound for some).
>
> **Art. 8 SFDR products** (promoting environmental or social characteristics): amount of "sustainable investments" in such products can in principle range from none or almost none to substantial amounts or even 100%. ESMA advises against the use of terms "sustainable" or "sustainability" in such products' names if they do not commit to a minimum proportion of "sustainable investments" – although the SFDR regulation as such does not contain legal grounds to prohibit such practice – "in order to avoid confusion with investors"[10].

(continue next page)

---

[9] SFDR Q&A 7/2021, p. 8.

[10] ESMA supervisory briefing 5/2022, p. 9.

(Overview continued)

> **Art. 9 SFDR products** (sustainable investments as objective): shall generally consist only of "sustainable investments" (with some narrow-defined exceptions permitted in order "to meet requirements in accordance with prudential, product-related specific rules … for certain specific purposes such as hedging or liquidity").[11]

As already indicated above, no market convention seems to have yet emerged with regard to Art. 7 SFDR products. Those products are increasingly defined as products considering PASI and it remains to be seen how the market practice regarding this product category will evolve. Due to the introduction of this sustainability preference category, not only the role of Art. 7 SFDR product level PASI disclosures, but also the role of entity level PASI disclosures under Art. 4 SFDR may continue to gain importance.

---

[11] SFDR Q&A 7/2021, p. 5.

VI. More Data for More ESG: The New Corporate Sustainability Reporting Directive

1. Importance of Quality ESG Data for the Sustainable Finance Effort

As the modern sustainable finance effort puts an ever stronger emphasis on companies' and their products' impact on the environment and society, it becomes increasingly clear that the effort cannot be successful without quality ESG data. And more of it. This important observation was put into a catchy phrase on LinkedIn recently by Deutsche Bundesbank's board member Sabine Mauderer: *"No data – no sustainable finance."*[1] This statement was made on the occasion of the International Conference on Statistics for Sustainable Finance, jointly organised by the Bank of France, Deutsche Bundesbank and the Irving Fisher Committee on Central Bank Statistics in Paris on 14 September 2021. At the current stage of sustainable finance market development, the availability of quality ESG data indeed pose a major practical challenge. Due to its complexity, importance and related practical challenges, ESG data could be a topic for a separate paper. The purpose of this section to give brief overview of how the enactment of the CSRD contributes to addressing the challenge under the European Sustainable Finance Action Plan's legislative agenda.

The European legislators and regulators undoubtedly understand the importance of ESG data and corporate sustainability reporting as its primary source for the sustainable finance effort. We have already outlined in the above sections that both SFDR and the Taxonomy Regulation entail provisions on entity level sustainability reporting. Those provisions are Art. 4 SFDR on entity level PASI reporting and Art. 8 Taxonomy Regulation on Taxonomy-alignment reporting for large firms falling under the scope of non-financial statement obligations under the Non-Financial Reporting Directive ("NFRD").

---

[1] LinkedIn post by Dr. Sabine Mauderer, Member of the Executive Board of the the Deutsche Bundesbank on the occasion of the International Conference on Statistics for Sustainable Finance, jointly organised by the Bank of France, Deutsche Bundesbank and the Irving Fisher Committee on Central Bank Statistics, Paris, 14 September 2021 (available at: <https://de.linkedin.com/posts/sabine-mauderer-7688327_data-finance-sustainable-activity-6843490948400324608-1XwT?trk=public_profile_like_view>, last visited on January 15, 2023).

2. Context and Starting Point:
NFRD's "Old" Corporate ESG Reporting Regime

In Section IV.4. on Taxonomy Regulation and its interplay with the Non-Financial Reporting Directive, we have already shown that the Taxonomy Regulation's requirement of Art. 8 ("Transparency of undertakings in non-financial statements") is phrased in such a way that it references to NFRD for defining its personal scope of application. We have also outlined Taxonomy Regulation's additional requirements on Taxonomy-alignment reporting for firms falling under NFRD's personal scope of application for non-financial statement requirement as per Art. 19a NFRD ("Non-financial statement") and Art. 29a NFRD ("Consolidated non-financial statement"). Accordingly, the *NFRD's personal scope of application as relates to the personal scope of application of its non-financial statement requirements under the NFRD* plays a key role in the EU's sustainable finance effort. The "old" Non-Financial Reporting Directive's Art. 19a and Art. 29a personal scope of application covered large public-interest entities with *more than 500 employees*. According to the European Commission's Explanatory memorandum to the CSRD draft[2] and its website information dedicated to corporate sustainability reporting[3], "this *covers approximately 11'700 large companies and groups* across the EU, including listed companies, banks, insurance companies, other companies designated by national authorities as public-interest entities" (emphasis added). Under the new CSRD standard, as per the European Commission's estimates, the number of firms having to report on sustainability *shall grow to "approximately 50'000 companies in total"*.

Information to be disclosed in company's/group's non-financial statement as part of management report as per Art. 19a(1)/Art. 29a(1) NFRD had to include, as a minimum, information on *environmental, social and employee matters, respect for human rights, anti-corruption and bribery matters*. This had to be done "to the extent necessary for an understanding of the undertaking's development, performance, position and impact of its activity" relating to the above-mentioned topics. On its website dedicated to this topic, the European Commission also emphases the importance of disclosures on "diversity on company boards (in terms of age, gender, educational and professional background)." In 2017 and 2019, the European Commission published non-mandatory guidelines on, respectively, environmental and social information disclosures as well as climate-related information reporting. As the

---

[2] Explanatory memorandum to the CSRD proposal draft 4/2021, p. 1.

[3] Available at: <https://finance.ec.europa.eu/capital-markets-union-and-financial-markets/company-reporting-and-auditing/company-reporting/corporate-sustainability-reporting_en>, last visited on January 15, 2023.

European Commission notes in its Explanatory memorandum to CSRD proposal draft, "these guidelines have not sufficiently improved the quality of information companies disclose pursuant to the NFRD."[4]

3. Laying the Foundation for CSRD: The Action Plan's "Fitness Check" of NFRD

Under the Sustainable Finance Action Plan's legislative agenda – Action category 3: "Fostering transparency and long-termism", Action item 9: "Strengthening sustainability disclosure and accounting rule-making" – it was foreseen to conduct a NFRD "fitness check" and make a proposal for a Corporate Sustainability Reporting Directive in order to make Europe's corporate sustainability regime suitable to fulfil its role under the Europe's new sustainable finance regulatory architecture.

The draft proposal of the envisaged Corporate Sustainability Reporting Directive was adopted by the European Commission on 21 April 2021, as part of the "April 2021 Package" in sustainable finance. As per European Commission's website information regarding the role of CSRD proposal, the CSRD aims to "amend the existing reporting requirements of the NFRD" and extend its scope to "all large companies and all companies listed on regulated markets (except listed micro-enterprises)". That extension shall happen gradually as the new wording of Art. 19a NFRD indicated[5] and final adopted text of the CSRD now confirms.

In its Q&A on the occasion of the publication of CSRD's proposal draft[6], the European Commission emphasizes that the CSRD will extend the scope of the existing NFRD corporate sustainability reporting requirements "to include all large companies, whether they are listed or not and without the previous 500-employee threshold."[7] The document also explains that the purpose of such proposed change is to make all large companies "publicly accountable for their *impact* on people and the environment (emphasis added)." The European Commission is also of the view that such changes broadening the sustainability reporting scope "responds to demands from investors for sustainability information from such companies." Very importantly, the European Commission notes that the changes also partly driven by investor protection considerations and stresses that, for reasons of investor protection, "it is especially important that investors have access to sustaina-

---

[4] CSRD proposal draft 4/2021, p. 1.
[5] CSRD proposal draft 4/2021, p. 42 (Art. 19a NFRD replacement).
[6] EC Q&A CSRD proposal 4/2021.
[7] EC Q&A CSRD proposal 4/2021, Section on Scope.

3. Laying the Foundation for CSRD

bility information from listed companies." The Commission is also of the that view that, due to changing market environment, "if listed SMEs do not report sustainability information, they may find themselves at risk of exclusion from investment portfolios" and that this risk "will grow as sustainability information becomes ever more important throughout the financial system." The document further states that "many SMEs are facing growing requests for sustainability information – typically from banks that lend them money and large companies that they supply."[8] The new reporting standards would "help SMEs play a full role in transition to a sustainable economy." The Q&A document further observes that changes proposed by CSRD draft are necessary "to ensure alignment with other EU initiatives on sustainable finance, in particular the Sustainable Finance Disclosure Regulation (SFDR) and the Taxonomy Regulation."[9] As to the rising costs of reporting, the Q&A document states that "most companies will face an increase in costs anyway because of growing demand from investors and other stakeholders for corporate sustainability information."[10]

It is worth noting that the European Commission's Explanatory memorandum reminds of and (re)emphasizes the importance of the principle of "double materiality" for the EU's sustainability reporting regime under NFRD[11]:

> "The NFRD introduced a requirement for companies to report both on how sustainability issues affect their performance, position and development (the '*outside-in*' *perspective*), and on their impact on people and the environment (the '*inside-out*' *perspective*). This is often known as '*double materiality*'."

This principle plays an increasingly important role in modern sustainable finance debate shaped by the legislative agenda of the Sustainable Finance Action Plan, with the principle's key conceptual role being once more reemphasized by the new Sustainable Finance Strategy[12]. This aspect is particularly highlighted also in European Commission's already quoted Q&A on CSRD draft[13], which states that "EU sustainability reporting standards need to be consistent with the European Green Deal and with Europe's existing legal framework, the Sustainable Finance Disclosure Regulation and the Taxonomy Regulation". All of them need to cover "*not just the risks* to companies *but also the impacts* of companies on society and the environment (the so-called 'double materiality' principle)", at the same time emphasizing the

---

[8] EC Q&A CSRD proposal 4/2021, Section on SMEs.

[9] EC Q&A CSRD proposal 4/2021, Section on Coherence.

[10] EC Q&A CSRD proposal 4/2021, Section on Costs.

[11] Explanatory memorandum to CSRD proposal draft 4/2021, p. 1. Emphasis added.

[12] Sustainable Finance Strategy, pp. 3, 11.

[13] EC Q&A CSRD proposal 4/2021.

importance that the European sustainability reporting standards are "globally aligned".[14]

The Explanatory memorandum to CSRD draft proposal also emphasizes the importance of interplay of various corporate reporting provisions under the new European sustainable finance regulatory framework:[15]

> "The NFRD, together with the Sustainable Finance Disclosure Regulation (SFDR) and the Taxonomy Regulation, are the central components of the sustainability reporting requirements underpinning the EU's sustainable finance strategy. The purpose of this legal framework is to create a consistent and coherent flow of sustainability information throughout the financial value chain."

The CSRD proposal "builds on and revises the sustainability reporting requirements set out in the NFRD, in order to make sustainability reporting requirements more consistent with the broader sustainable finance legal framework, including the SFDR and the Taxonomy Regulation, and to tie in with the objectives of the European Green Deal."

4. CSRD: Europe's New Corporate Sustainability Reporting Regime

The CSRD has been formally adopted in November 2022 and published in the EU Official Journal on the 16th of December 2022. As envisaged, it gradually extends the corporate sustainability reporting duties to an ever larger spectrum of companies, broadens the scope of matters to be reported on and thus will feed the market with ever more sustainability-related information needed to make investment decisions enabling the transition to a more sustainable economy.

Conceptual evolution: from "non-financial" to "sustainability". The CSRD marks a major step in conceptual evolution of the area which is mostly still called "non-financial" corporate reporting by (too) many. On the regulatory front, it marks the end of generally qualifying corporate ESG reporting as "non-financial" and indicates a shift in how reporting on sustainability matters will be seen going forward. The choice of words and thus a switch in title of the overall EU Directive 2022/2464 of 14 December 2022 – which among other laws also changes the *Non-Financial* Reporting Directive as that legislative package's key item – to Corporate *Sustainability* Reporting Directive gives a clear sign of this conceptual shift, but is easy to oversee if one is too focused on the technicalities of corporate reporting alone. Also the new title of Article 19a of the amended Directive 2013/34/EU reflects this

---

[14] EC Q&A CSRD proposal 4/2021, Section on International. Emphasis added.
[15] Explanatory memorandum to CSRD proposal draft 4/2021 (section on "Consistency with existing policy provisions in the policy are"). Emphasis added.

4. CSRD: Europe's New Corporate Sustainability Reporting Regime 73

conceptual change (old version of that article was titled "Non-financial statement"). Recital 8 CSRD clarifies the logic underlying this conceptual change:

> "Many stakeholders consider the term 'non-financial' to be inaccurate, in particular because it implies that the information in question has no financial relevance. Increasingly, however, such information does have financial relevance. Many organisations, initiatives and practitioners in the field of sustainability reporting refer to 'sustainability information'. It is therefore preferable to use the term 'sustainability information' in place of 'non- financial information'. Directive 2013/34/EU should therefore be amended to take account of that change in terminology."

This terminological change suits well into the EUAP regulatory framework, especially next to the SFDR as it dominant piece in practice, which aims at creating comparable levels of sustainability-related transparency on product level as the CSRD does on corporate level. Both the title of the SFDR (i.e. that fact that it is called *Sustainable Finance* Disclosure Regulation and not *Non-Financial* Disclosure Regulation) and well as how the regulation defines the term "sustainability risk" as its key concept indicates at least in part that the key concepts at the core of it are not considered being "non-financial" by the legislator. Farewell to the terminology of the old era (i.e. talking of "sustainability" rather than "non-financial") may be not as "noticeable" under the SFDR as it is under the CSRD, but its impact on practice is likely to be not less significant. Beside taking on the technical CSRD implementation challenges, conceptualizing the impact of this evolution in how we think about sustainability will certainly require substantial effort in coming years both in practice and academia.

The requirement of the new Art. 19a(1) of the amended Directive 2013/34/EU to publish sustainability information as part of the management report (in a dedicated, clearly identifiable section), removing the previously existing option of publishing the information in a separate report, shall be seen as part of the same conceptual shift. As Recital 57 CSRD explains:

> "Publication in a separate report can also give the impression, internally and externally, that sustainability information belongs to a category of less relevant information, which can impact negatively on the perceived reliability of the information. Undertakings should therefore report sustainability information in a clearly identifiable dedicated section of the management report and Member States should no longer be allowed to exempt undertakings from the obligation to include in the management report information on sustainability matters."

Broadening the reporting's substantive scope. Compared to NFRD, the CSRD marks an evolution in terms of what is understood as "sustainability matters" relevant for corporate reporting purposes. It is the scope of those matters taken together with the level of required detail and nuance in corporate reporting which marks a substantial step forward compared to the NFRD standard. As its foundation and key reference point, the CSRD takes reference to SFDR's definition of "sustainability factors", emphasizes importance of alignment with that definition, while making clear that that SFDR's definition does not explicitly include governance matters – "G" under "ESG" – and underscoring that the definition of "sustainability matters" under CSRD shall cover that important element as well.[16]

Recital 28 CSRD provides further useful guidance on the role of "E", "S" and "G" und thus the concept of "ESG" in European sustainable finance regulatory context, officially positioning it as reflecting the needs and expectations of users and undertakings and thus recognizing its role as a practical tool of operationalizing the rather abstract concept of sustainability in practice of corporate sustainability reporting:

> "That list should also correspond to the needs and expectations of users and undertakings, who often use the terms *'environmental'*, *'social'* and *'governance'* as a means of categorising the *three main sustainability matters*. ..." (*emphasis added*)

"Sustainability matters" – CSRD's definition

New Art. 2(17) amended Directive 2013/34/EU: "sustainability matters" means environmental, social and human rights, *and governance* factors, including sustainability factors defined in point (24) of Article 2 of Regulation (EU) 2019/2088 [=SFDR]; (*emphasis added*)

"Sustainability factors" – SFDR's definition

Art. 2(24) SFDR: 'sustainability factors' mean environmental, social and employee matters, respect for human rights, anti-corruption and anti-bribery matters.

The expanded list of sustainability matters to be reported under the new CSRD corporate sustainability reporting standard covers the following areas:

– *General:* information necessary to understand 1) undertaking's impact on sustainability matters and 2) how sustainability matters affect undertaking's development, performance and position;

– *Business model and strategy:* 1) resilience of business model and strategy in relation to sustainability matters-related risks; 2) sustainability matters-related opportunities; 3) plan and implementing actions regarding Paris-aligned transition and net zero 2050 target, exposure to fossil fuel activities; 4) taking into account of stakeholders' interests and impacts on sustainability matters; 5) implementation of the sustainability matters-related strategy;

---

[16] See Recital 28 CSRD.

4. CSRD: Europe's New Corporate Sustainability Reporting Regime

- *Time-bound sustainability matters-related targets* such as absolute greenhouse gas emission reduction targets at least for 2030 and 2050, including progress and whether targets are based on conclusive scientific evidence;
- *Role of administrative, management and supervisory bodies* regarding sustainability matters, including their own expertise and skills in this area or access to bodies with such expertise;
- *Policies* in relation to sustainability matters;
- *Incentive schemes* linked to sustainability matters offered to administrative, management and supervisory bodies;
- *Due diligence process* regarding 1) sustainability matters; 2) principal actual or potential adverse impacts connected to undertaking's own operations and value chain, including products and services, business relationships and supply chain, actions taken to identify and monitor those impacts; 3) actions taken to prevent, mitigate, remediate or end actual or potential adverse impacts, including results of such actions;
- *Principal risks* related to sustainability matters, including principal dependencies and how undertaking manages them;
- *Indicators relevant* for all the above points;
- *Process carried out to identify* information reported as per points above.

Information box below gives the relevant text excerpt from the CSRD provision dedicated to the scope of sustainability reporting.

"Sustainability matters" to be reported under the new CSRD standard

Amended Directive 2013/34/EU Article 19a: Sustainability reporting (excerpt)

1. Large undertakings, and small and medium-sized undertakings, except micro undertakings, which are public- interest entities as defined in point (a) of point (1) of Article 2 shall include in the management report information necessary to understand the undertaking's impacts on sustainability matters, and information necessary to understand how sustainability matters affect the undertaking's development, performance and position.

The information referred to in the first subparagraph shall be clearly identifiable within the management report, through a dedicated section of the management report.

2. The information referred to in paragraph 1 shall contain:

(a) a brief description of the undertaking's business model and strategy, including:

(i) the resilience of the undertaking's business model and strategy in relation to risks related to sustainability matters;

(ii) the opportunities for the undertaking related to sustainability matters;

(continue next page)

(iii) the plans of the undertaking, including implementing actions and related financial and investment plans, to ensure that its business model and strategy are compatible with the transition to a sustainable economy and with the limiting of global warming to 1,5 °C in line with the Paris Agreement under the United Nations Framework Convention on Climate Change adopted on 12 December 2015 (the 'Paris Agreement') and the objective of achieving climate neutrality by 2050 as established in Regulation (EU) 2021/1119 of the European Parliament and of the Council (*), and, where relevant, the exposure of the undertaking to coal-, oil- and gas-related activities;

(iv) how the undertaking's business model and strategy take account of the interests of the undertaking's stakeholders and of the impacts of the undertaking on sustainability matters;

(v) how the undertaking's strategy has been implemented with regard to sustainability matters;

(b) a description of the time-bound targets related to sustainability matters set by the undertaking, including, where appropriate, absolute greenhouse gas emission reduction targets at least for 2030 and 2050, a description of the progress the undertaking has made towards achieving those targets, and a statement of whether the undertaking's targets related to environmental factors are based on conclusive scientific evidence;

(c) a description of the role of the administrative, management and supervisory bodies with regard to sustainability matters, and of their expertise and skills in relation to fulfilling that role or the access such bodies have to such expertise and skills;

(d) a description of the undertaking's policies in relation to sustainability matters;

(e) information about the existence of incentive schemes linked to sustainability matters which are offered to members of the administrative, management and supervisory bodies;

(f) a description of:

(i) the due diligence process implemented by the undertaking with regard to sustainability matters, and, where applicable, in line with Union requirements on undertakings to conduct a due diligence process;

(ii) the principal actual or potential adverse impacts connected with the undertaking's own operations and with its value chain, including its products and services, its business relationships and its supply chain, actions taken to identify and monitor those impacts, and other adverse impacts which the undertaking is required to identify pursuant to other Union requirements on undertakings to conduct a due diligence process;

(iii) any actions taken by the undertaking to prevent, mitigate, remediate or bring an end to actual or potential adverse impacts, and the result of such actions;

(g) a description of the principal risks to the undertaking related to sustainability matters, including a description of the undertaking's principal dependencies on those matters, and how the undertaking manages those risks;

(continue next page)

4. CSRD: Europe's New Corporate Sustainability Reporting Regime

> (h) indicators relevant to the disclosures referred to in points (a) to (g).
>
> Undertakings shall report the process carried out to identify the information that they have included in the management report in accordance with paragraph 1 of this Article. The information listed in the first subparagraph of this paragraph shall include (...) information related to short-, medium- and long-term time horizons, as applicable.

A special, simplified regime is foreseen for SMEs (see Art. 19a(6)–(7)), with a possibility to opt out from it until 2028.

CSRD's outline of key items to be covered under the upcoming sustainability reporting standards serves as a good general guidance on what falls under "E", "S" and "G" under European corporate sustainability reporting standard as part of the European Sustainable Finance Action Plan's new regulatory framework for sustainable finance:[17]

Key elements of "E", "S" and "G" under new CSRD's reporting standard – CSRD's outline		
"E"	"S"	"G"
– climate change mitigation, including as regards scope 1, scope 2 and, where relevant, scope 3 greenhouse gas emissions; – climate change adaptation; – water and marine resources; – Resource use and the circular economy; – pollution; – biodiversity and ecosystems.	– equal treatment and opportunities for all, including gender equality and equal pay for work of equal value, training and skills development, the employment and inclusion of people with disabilities, measures against violence and harassment in the workplace, and diversity; – working conditions, including secure employment, working time, adequate wages, social dialogue, freedom of association, existence of works councils, collective bargaining, including the proportion of workers covered by	– the role of the undertaking's administrative, management and supervisory bodies with regard to sustainability matters, and their composition, as well as their expertise and skills in relation to fulfilling that role or the access such bodies have to such expertise and skills; – the main features of the undertaking's internal control and risk management systems, in relation to the sustainability reporting and decision-making process;

(continue next page)

---

[17] See newly inserted Chapter's 6a Art. 29b "Sustainability reporting standards" of the amended Directive 2013/34/EU.

"E"	"S"	"G"
	collective agreements, the information, consultation and participation rights of workers, work-life balance, and health and safety; – respect for the human rights, fundamental freedoms, democratic principles and standards established in the International Bill of Human Rights and other core UN human rights conventions, including the UN Convention on the Rights of Persons with Disabilities, the UN Declaration on the Rights of Indigenous Peoples, the International Labour Organization's Declaration on Fundamental Principles and Rights at Work and the fundamental conventions of the International Labour Organization, the European Convention for the protection of Human Rights and Fundamental Freedoms, the European Social Charter, and the Charter of Fundamental Rights of the European Union.	– business ethics and corporate culture, including anti-corruption and anti-bribery, the protection of whistleblowers and animal welfare; – activities and commitments of the undertaking related to exerting its political influence, including its lobbying activities; – the management and quality of relationships with customers, suppliers and communities affected by the activities of the undertaking, including payment practices, especially with regard to late payment to small and medium-sized undertakings.

Special emphasis on "double materiality". Recital 29 CSRD explicitly (re)emphasizes the importance of the principle of the so-called "double materiality". The principle of "double materiality" refers to reporting "*not only* on information to the extent necessary for an understanding of the undertaking's development, performance and position, *but also* on information necessary for an understanding of the impact of the undertaking's activities on environmental, social and employee matters, respect for human rights, anti-corruption and bribery matters". That same Recital 29 CSRD also notes that while the principle of double materiality itself was known under the "old" Euro-

4. CSRD: Europe's New Corporate Sustainability Reporting Regime 79

pean corporate ESG reporting standard, it was apparently often not well understood and applied, which CSRD shall correct:

> "Those Articles [Article 19a(1) and Article 29a(1) of Directive 2013/34/EU] therefore require undertakings to report both on the impacts of the activities of the undertaking on people and the environment, and on how sustainability matters affect the undertaking. That is referred to as the double materiality perspective, in which the risks to the undertaking and the impacts of the undertaking each represent one materiality perspective. *The fitness check on corporate reporting shows that those two perspectives are often not well understood or applied. It is therefore necessary to clarify that undertakings should consider each materiality perspective in its own right*, and should disclose information that is material from both perspectives as well as information that is material from only one perspective."

This emphasis on the importance of the "double materiality" principle for purposes of corporate ESG reporting is in line with the European Commission's focus on the importance of this principle for the overall EU's sustainable finance effort as reflected in its Sustainable Finance Strategy of 2021.

Enhancing the level of assurance for ESG data. Taking note of the rapidly growing market for sustainability information, Recital 10 CSRD voices the legislator's expectation that the CSRD's amendments to Directive 2013/34/EU "are expected to increase the comparability of data and harmonise standards." Recital 11 CSRD further observes "a very significant increase in demand for corporate sustainability information in recent years", particularly in the investment community. This is partly driven by the "changing nature of risks to undertakings" as well as "growing investor awareness of the financial implications of those risks". In this context, the CSRD emphasizes the importance of climate-related financial risks. Recital 11 CSRD further notes that the "increase in demand for sustainability information is also driven by the growth in investment products that explicitly seek to meet certain sustainability standards or achieve certain sustainability objectives and to ensure coherence with the ambition" (such as, for example the Paris agreement). Though noting that the increase in demand can be seen as logical consequences of the adoption of the SFDR and Taxonomy Regulation, the legislator is of the view that "some of that increase would have happened in any case, due to fast-changing citizen awareness, consumer preferences and market practices."

In context of these developments and while discussing the findings of the NFRD's "fitness check" for EUAP purposes, Recital 13 CSRD explains that "there is a clear need for a *robust and affordable reporting framework* that is *accompanied by effective auditing practices to ensure the reliability of data* and *avoid greenwashing* and double counting" (emphasis added). After explaining the difference between "limited assurance engagements" and "reasonable assurance engagements", emphasizing the importance of assurance requirement for sustainability reporting in order to not threaten the credibility of the sustainability information disclosed, Recital 60 CSRD makes clear that the objective of the legislator is to "have similar level of assurance for financial and sustainability reporting". However, what is currently missing is a "commonly agreed standard for sustainability reporting." CSRD foresees "a progressive approach to enhancing the level of the assurance required for sustainability information", with the adoption of assurance standards for reasonable assurance of sustainability reporting scheduled to happen by "no later than 1 October 2028", following a practical feasibility assessment on both auditors' and undertakings' side. Recital 61 CSRD reminds that auditors "already verify the financial statements and the management report." The legislator is of the view that the "assurance of sustainability reporting by the statutory auditors or audit firms would help to ensure the connectivity between, and consistency of, financial and sustainability information, which is particularly important for users of sustainability information."

Key element of the Action Plan's anti-greenwashing effort. Though the CSRD does not include its own definition of greenwashing, the directive is intended to play an important role in new European sustainable finance regulatory architecture's anti-greenwashing effort.[18] Two of CSRD's recitals address the phenomenon of greenwashing:

- Recital 2 CSRD, discussing the Sustainable Finance Action Plan's legislative action items, reminds that the Taxonomy Regulation "creates a classification system of environmentally sustainable economic activities *with the aim of* scaling up sustainable investments and *combatting greenwashing* of financial products that *unduly claim to be sustainable*" (emphasis added). As explained in Section IV.4., EU's corporate ESG reporting regime in the form of NFRD, as "upgraded" by the CSRD is closely interlinked with the Taxonomy Regulation, via the instrument of Art. 8 Taxonomy Regulation.

- Discussing NFRD's "fitness check" for the purposes of Sustainable Finance Action Plan, Recital 13 CSRD explains that "there is a clear need for a robust and affordable reporting framework that is accompanied by effective auditing practices to *ensure the reliability of data* and *avoid greenwashing* and double counting."

Under the header "Addressing greenwashing", the Sustainable Finance Strategy of 2021 explicitly lists (next to the Taxonomy Regulation and the SFDR), the proposed CSRD as part of the EU's disclosure regime created "to prevent greenwashing" and, through the increased level of transparency,

---

[18] For further details on the EU's anti-greenwashing effort in sustainable finance, see Section VII.

help investors to identify "credible investment opportunities".[19] Accordingly, the CSRD's enactment closes the circle under the Sustainable Finance Action Plan's legislative agenda also in the increasingly important field of tackling greenwashing.

Extending the personal scope of application. Extending a law's personal scope of application might seem like a formality, but the move's effects in case of the CSRD on the ESG data market are expected to be of major impact: the reporting duty will be extended from approximately 11.700 to approximately 50.000 firms, filling the sustainable finance market with the much-required corporate sustainability/ESG data. The plan to reach third-country firms with significant activity on the EU's territory means that the new reporting standard will likely gain in relevance also outside of Europe. Market's voluntary take-up of the EU's new corporate sustainability reporting standard is another field where important developments can be expected in the coming years.

Gradual go-live. As per EU Council's press release of 21 June 2022 announcing provisional political agreement between the Council and the European Parliament on CSRD, it is envisaged that the go-live of the regulation will take place in three stages.[20] This pre-announced timeline has been confirmed in the final text of the CSRD as published in the EU Official Journal on the 16 December 2022. The corporate sustainability reporting obligation according to CSRD will start applying according to the following timeline:

- 1 January 2024 for companies already subject to the NFRD, i.e. large public-interest companies with over 500 employees (with first reports due in 2025, for financial year 2024);
- 1 January 2025 for large companies that are not presently subject to the NFRD, i.e. companies exceeding two of the following three criteria: 250 employees; € 40 million in turnover; € 20 million in total assets;
- 1 January 2026 for listed SMEs and other undertakings in scope;
- Transition period until 2028: an opt-out possible for SMEs.

It needs to be noted that certain third country-undertakings with significant activity on the EU's territory will fall under the scope of CSRD reporting duty and will have to deliver a sustainability report according to the reporting standards to be adopted by the European Commission by 30 June 2024.

Furthermore, Recital 21 para 2 CSRD explicitly highlights the possibility and optionality of voluntary reporting.

---

[19] Sustainable Finance Strategy, p. 16.
[20] EU Council Press Release on CSRD 6/2022.

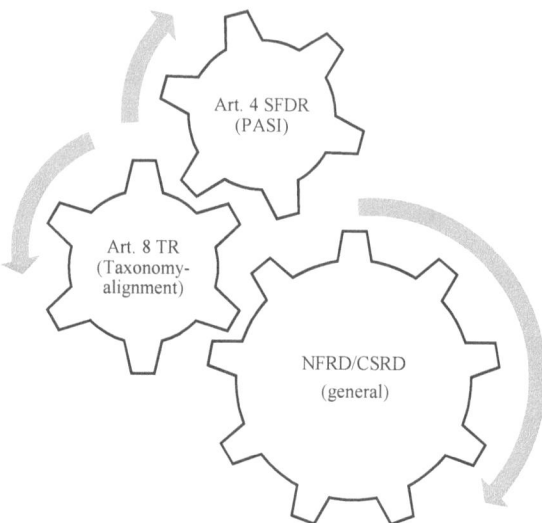

Figure: Overview – Key components corporate sustainability reporting

The above figure gives a general overview of central elements in Europe's sustainability reporting regime, focusing on Level 1 provisions, while it need to be kept in mind that substantial level of detail and quantitative elements are/will be added to that by Level 2 acts (both on Art. 4 SFDR as well as on Art. 8 TR), which are in process of gradual application roll-out.

The SFDR/TR final RTS, in form of the Commission's Delegated Regulation (EU) 2022/1288 of 6 April 2022, which includes detailed provisions and a dedicated template in form of Annex 1 on Art. 4 SFDR PASI reporting, has been published in the Official Journal of the European Union on 25 July 2022 and has started applying from 1 January 2023,[21] while the delegated act supplementing Art. 8 TR and specifying contents and presentation of Taxonomy-alignment information for company's subject to Art. 19a and 29a NFRD was already in force and applicable from 1 January 2022. In this context, it

---

[21] Commission Delegated Regulation (EU) 2022/1288 of 6 April 2022 supplementing Regulation (EU) 2019/2088 of the European Parliament and of the Council with regard to regulatory technical standards specifying the details of the content and presentation of the information in relation to the principle of 'do no significant harm', specifying the content, methodologies and presentation of information in relation to sustainability indicators and adverse sustainability impacts, and the content and presentation of the information in relation to the promotion of environmental or social characteristics and sustainable investment objectives in pre-contractual documents, on websites and in periodic reports, OJ L 196, pp. 1–72.

4. CSRD: Europe's New Corporate Sustainability Reporting Regime

is worth noting that such established voluntary global corporate responsibility frameworks from the "pre-Action-Plan"-era as the UN Global Compact of 2000[22] seem to be in process of reinventing themselves as corporate sustainability reporting regimes, which adds complexity in terms of *moving parts* to the already complex and fast-evolving regulatory landscape for sustainability.

---

[22] UN Global Compact, The Ten Principles, 2000.

VII. Tackling Greenwashing

The disclosure requirements under the Sustainable Finance Action Plan are introduced to help preventing greenwashing[1]. A common definition of sustainability introduced under the Action Plan's legislative agenda shall also provide "protection against greenwashing."[2] While the first regulatory definitions of greenwashing under Sustainable Finance Action Plan's regulatory framework have started to emerge before the publication of the EU's Sustainability Finance Strategy in July 2021,[3] it seems that it was with that publication when everyone's focus started to turn to the objective of tackling greenwashing. Besides adding its own definition of greenwashing[4], the Strategy emphasizes that "the effectiveness of sustainable finance policies also depends on an adequate level of enforcement across the EU"[5]. Five definitions of the regulatory concept of greenwashing under EU sustainable finance law have emerged in the meantime, as presented in the analysis of Zukas/Trafkowski[6] (see overview table below). Here, it needs to be noted that SFDR/TR RTS published in final form on 25 July 2022 take over the definition of greenwashing as it was known under the February 2021 SFDR L2 RTS draft, right in parallel with MiFID II changes introducing the concept of client's sustainability preferences going live.

---

[1] Sustainable Finance Strategy, p. 16.
[2] Sustainable Finance Strategy, p. 3.
[3] For an in-depth overview, see *Zukas/Trafkowski*.
[4] Sustainable Finance Strategy, p. 3, fn. 11 (greenwashing: "The use of marketing to portray an organisation's products, activities or policies as environmentally friendly when they are not").
[5] Sustainable Finance Strategy, p. 17.
[6] *Zukas/Trafkowski*, pp. 3, 13.

4. CSRD: Europe's New Corporate Sustainability Reporting Regime

#	Definition	Source	Date
1	"greenwashing refers to the practice of gaining an unfair competitive advantage by marketing a financial product as *environmentally friendly*, when in fact *basic environmental standards* have not been met."	Taxonomy Regulation	2020/6
2	"'greenwashing' ... is, in particular, the practice of gaining an unfair competitive advantage by recommending a financial product as *environmentally friendly or sustainable*, when in fact that financial product does not meet *basic environmental or other sustainability-related standards*."	SFDR/ TR RTS	2022/7
3	making "unsubstantiated sustainability claims"; "the use of marketing to portray an organisation's products, activities or policies as *environmentally friendly when they are not*."	Sustainable Finance Strategy	2021/7
4	"conveying a false impression, or providing misleading information about *how* a financial product is performing in terms of *ESG sustainability*."	EC SFDR Q&A	2021/7
5	"the practice of gaining an unfair competitive advantage by recommending a financial instrument as *environmentally friendly or sustainable*, when in fact that financial instrument does not meet *basic environmental or other sustainability-related standards*."	MiFID II delegated act	2021/8

Overview – Greenwashing definitions[7]

Based on the analysis and findings of Zukas/Trafkowski[8], the key elements of the definition of greenwashing under the EU's sustainable finance regulations can be grouped as follows:

Key elements – regulatory concept of greenwashing/EU sustainable finance[9]
1. *General elements*: practice of gaining "unfair competitive advantage" (Taxonomy Regulation, SFDR/TR RTS, MiFID II delegated act), making "unsubstantiated ESG claims" (Sustainable Finance Strategy);
2. *Activities in scope*: marketing (Taxonomy Regulation, Sustainable Finance Strategy), recommending (SFDR/TR RTS, MiFID II delegated act), performance reporting (EC SFDR Q&A);

---

[7] Table adapted from (updated): *Zukas/Trafkowski*, p. 13.
[8] *Zukas/Trafkowski*.
[9] Overview adapted from (updated): *Zukas/Trafkowski*, pp. 12–13.

> 3. *Relevant offerings, corporate communication*: financial products (Taxonomy Regulation, SFDR RTS, EC SFDR Q&A); organisation's products, activities, policies (Sustainable Finance Strategy); financial instruments (MiFID II delegated act);
> 4. *Claims in scope*: "environmentally friendly" (Taxonomy Regulation, Sustainable Finance Strategy); "environmentally friendly or sustainable" (SFDR/TR RTS, MiFID II delegated act); "ESG sustainability" (EC SFDR Q&A);
> 5. *Relevant standards*: "basic environmental" (Taxonomy Regulation), "basic environmental or other sustainability-related" (SFDR/TR RTS, MiFID II delegated act).

The increasing focus on greenwashing prevention has been confirmed in the ESMA's 2022 Annual Work Programme published in September 2021[10]. Following that, ESMA sent a very clear signal starting the year 2022 by publishing its Sustainable Finance Roadmap 2022–2024, which listed fight against greenwashing as its priority number one for the coming three years ("Tackling greenwashing and promoting transparency")[11]. Adding to the 5 regulatory definitions of greenwashing known under EU sustainable finance law until then, the Sustainable Finance Roadmap provides what it seems like an attempt to conceptualize the phenomenon of greenwashing on a more general level[12]:

> "The term greenwashing *may be defined in a number of ways*, but it intuitively refers to market practices, both *intentional and unintentional*, whereby the publicly disclosed *sustainability profile of an issuer* and the characteristics and/or objectives of a *financial instrument* or a *financial product* either by action or omission do not properly reflect the underlying sustainability risks and impacts associated to that issuer, financial instrument or financial product.
>
> As such, greenwashing typically gives rise to potential detriment to investors who wish to allocate resources to sustainable investments. Greenwashing could, therefore, be generally identified as a *misrepresentation, mislabelling, mis-selling and/or mis-pricing* phenomenon. However, *these terms may only represent the ultimate symptoms*, since the causes of greenwashing may relate to multiple aspects of the functioning of the investment value chain, sometimes affecting nodes of that chain long before a certain financial product reaches the final investor. This is the case, for example, of *issuers' disclosures misrepresenting the real sustainability profile of a listed entity* or the *poor quality of data available to an EU investment fund on investee companies located within or outside the EU*." Emphasis added.

---

[10] ESMA 2022 Annual Work Programme, 27 September 2021, pp. 9–10.
[11] ESMA Roadmap 2022, p. 8.
[12] ESMA Roadmap 2022, p. 8, point 10 a.

This definition is undoubtedly broad and adds an important layer to the already existing ones summarized in the above-quoted study by Zukas/Trafkowski[13], with some elements, such as focus on gaining unfair competitive advantage or making unsubstantiated sustainability claims, which are at those definitions' core[14] being not reflected in the ESMA Roadmap's attempt to conceptualise it. On the other hand, the ESMA Roadmap gives useful insights into ESMA's thinking with regard to such important aspects as the intentionality, additional emphasis on publicly disclosed sustainability profile of an issuer (i. e. entity level disclosures/communication), role of omission, importance of sustainability risk and impact elements in disclosures. The Roadmap provides further useful observations into ESMA's thinking on the roots of the problem[15]:

> "… the combination of growing investor demand, a fast-evolving market and legislative/regulatory measures which can only apply with a certain time lag creates room for misalignment between demands for investments that can make a sustainability impact and the available investing opportunities marketed as sustainable. There are multiple consequences of this misalignment which can ultimately be reconnected to the risk of mis-selling. However, greenwashing does not necessarily originate only at the moment a product is offered to the final investors. In fact, different steps of the investment chain may well contribute to the ultimate misrepresentation of the real sustainability profile of a certain investment to the end investors."

Furthermore, the Roadmap states "this topic as a main supervisory risk" and notes that coordinated response at EU level is necessary to tackle it[16]. The Roadmap also observes that NCAs note that "there is *no common understanding of what greenwashing is*"[17]. As ESMA proceeds with its analysis of the greenwashing phenomenon, it lists its considerations and case scenario examples with greenwashing risk for the areas of asset management, investment services, corporate disclosure and benchmarks[18]. Those considerations show how broad ESMA's understanding of the greenwashing phenomenon is. ESMA notes the need of "*Arriving at a definition* of the greenwashing phenomenon" for purposes of driving supervisory work in a coordinated and efficient manner bases on clear rules across the EU[19]. This analysis is shared by the study of Zukas/Trafkowski which noted that while we have seen five definitions of greenwashing recently emerged in the framework of the new

---

[13] *Zukas/Trafkowski*.
[14] *Zukas/Trafkowski*, pp. 12–13.
[15] ESMA Roadmap 2022, p. 11, point 17.
[16] ESMA Roadmap 2022, p. 12.
[17] ESMA Roadmap 2022, p. 12, point 22. Emphasis added.
[18] ESMA Roadmap 2022, pp. 12–13, point 22.
[19] ESMA Roadmap, 2022, p. 12, point 24. Emphasis added.

European sustainable finance regulatory architecture and that these definitions share certain common core elements, there is no general, uniform and official definition of the regulatory greenwashing concept in sustainable finance.[20] Moreover, it needs to e added that the final version of CSRD as published in the EU Official Journal on 16 December 2022 now also includes Recital 13, which emphasizes the importance of reliability of corporate ESG data for purposes of preventing greenwashing.[21]

Signalling its seriousness about tackling the topic and understanding the phenomenon of greenwashing in-depth, in May 2022 the European Commission issued a request for input to the European Banking Authority (EBA), the European Insurance and Occupational Pensions Authority (EIOPA) and the European Securities and Markets Authority (ESMA) related to greenwashing risks and supervision of sustainable finance policies[22]. The paper includes valuable insights into the development of European Commissions thinking on the topic and the outcomes of that process are expected to provide valuable empirical insights.

The continued regulatory uncertainty on this important topic adds to the sometimes observed general tendency to call almost everything one does not like in sustainable finance practice "greenwashing". This tendency can sometimes be observed even among finance and sustainable finance experts. This simplified approach to such complex topic certainly does not help for the healthy development of sustainable finance market, especially as it is currently in phase of transition, based on the changing, fast-evolving regulatory landscape. It is essential that the process of developing proper understanding of greenwashing remains focused on legal core elements of the concept as they already exist in various legislative and regulatory items and documents under the Action Plan's new sustainable finance regulatory framework and accompanying official statements.

With the European Commission and ESMA signalling how seriously they take the tasks of understanding and tackling the greenwashing phenomenon, substantial amount of supervisory and perhaps even regulatory activity in this field may be expected in the coming few years, with a need to conceptualize it on the academic level. In their joint call for evidence on greenwashing of 15 November 2022, the European Supervisory Authorities (ESAs) indicated they will publish their first findings in form of an interim/progress

---

[20] *Zukas/Trafkowski*, pp. 14, 28.

[21] For further details on this aspect, see Section VI.4.

[22] European Commission, Request for input to the European Banking Authority (EBA), the European Insurance and Occupational Pensions Authority (EIOPA) and the European Securities and Markets Authority (ESMA) related to greenwashing risks and supervision of sustainable finance policies, May 2022.

report in May 2023, which will then be followed by a final report in May 2024.[23] The risk dimension of the topic become even more complex after it has been clarified that SFDR is not a labelling regime and thus positioning SFDR products as such as some kind of quality labels in the eyes investors poses an additional risk of greenwashing.[24]

---

[23] European Supervisory Authorities, ESAs Call for evidence on better understanding greenwashing, 22 November 2022, p. 2 (available at: <https://www.esma.europa.eu/press-news/consultations/esas-call-evidence-greenwashing>, last visited on January 15, 2023).

[24] *Ross*, p. 7; see also Section II.3. above.

VIII. Concluding Observations

Over the past several years, sustainable finance has not only continued its rapid development into a separate academic discipline within the broader area of finance, but also went from niche to mainstream in business practice. Today, world-leading universities are successfully running and establishing graduate programs, general continuing education and executive courses in sustainable finance. A vibrant community of practitioners, enthusiasts but also critical voices intensely debates general and particularly also regulatory developments in the ESG field. The emerging academic literature on sustainable finance and sustainable investing tries to not only describe the existing market practices, but also provide conceptual foundations to further develop them,[1] with renowned former central bankers adding their insights and conceptual observations on the topic in form of lectures and books admirable for their scope, depth and intellectual ambition[2]. Those conceptual foundations are particularly important if we understand the sustainable finance not only as a mere check-the-box exercise, but an effort or process, which shall lead "to increased investments in longer-term and sustainable activities" as the European Sustainable Finance Action Plan makes clear when defining the concept[3].

In parallel to that, the field is in process of experiencing a true regulatory tsunami. A phenomenon, which will take time to be properly reflected in legal coursebooks on banking and financial markets law, with notable and rare exceptions addressing this ongoing shift at least in part already now.[4] While the field of general legal studies has produced impressive works on the legal concept of sustainability and sustainable development[5], the current regulatory wave, its detailed and technical character requires attention of legal scholars also on the technical level of banking, financial services and general business law and regulation, with such new topics in this field as the regula-

---

[1] To name just a few examples from the emerging academic literature in this field, trying not only describe the existing market practices, but also provide conceptual foundations to further develop them: *Schoenmaker/Schramade*; *Silvola/Landau*.

[2] For illustration, see *Carney*, How We Get What We Value; *Carney*, Value(s).

[3] Sustainable Finance Action Plan, p. 2. See also Section II.3.

[4] *Alexander*, Chapter 13 on "Environmental Sustainability", pp. 347–373 and Chapter 15 on "Future Challenges for Banking Regulation", pp. 395–416.

[5] To list just a few illustrative examples (all in German): *Mathis*; *Gehne*; *Kahl*.

VIII. Concluding Observations

tory concept of greenwashing acquiring particular practical relevance and thus requiring legal analysis and conceptualization.[6] The field finds itself in transition also in the sense of evolving from an area dominated by self-regulation and voluntary initiatives to the field governed by "hard law", regulatory instruments which conceptually mostly fall into the area of administrative business law, with its functional interplay with and impact on general private and business law.

With the enactment of key action items under the European Union's Sustainable Finance Action Plan such as the Sustainable Finance Disclosure Regulation, the Taxonomy Regulation, the MiFID II delegated act on sustainability preferences as well as the Corporate Sustainability Reporting Directive, key pieces of the new European sustainable finance regulatory framework are now in place and start to be applied. The test of practice will show how successful the European Union's approach will be in terms of achieving real world results.

This contribution is an attempt to demonstrate the scope and technical detail of the wave of regulation transforming the world of finance in Europe. It is also an attempt to start conceptualizing the field, but also give an insight into this vibrant new area of practice, which is yet in process of finding its proper place in universities and coursebooks of banking, finance and general business law. The emerging field of sustainable finance law and regulation is in process of touching all aspects of finance business, from technical aspects of product and corporate reporting to such topics as strategy and corporate purpose. To fully grasp the impact of this rethinking of banking and business regulation and properly navigate the field, a holistic, specialized "master generalist" perspective is required, beside the absolutely necessary but narrower technical specialist perspective.

The recent critical report on ESG investing by the Economist suggested for the "term ESG to be scrapped" as it sounds "more like a pious mantra than a force for change."[7] At the same time, the report noted that the field of "sustainable investing is not about to disappear"[8], adding that "more regulation may make it more credible"[9] as "investors continue to care not just about returns but about the world they live it". The European regulator's effort to create a new regulatory framework for sustainable finance, which is

---

[6] For an effort in this direction, see *Zukas/Trafkowski*.

[7] The Economist Special Report, The future of ESG: Measure less, but better, p. 12.

[8] The Economist Special Report, The future of ESG: Measure less, but better, p. 12.

[9] The Economist Special Report, The future of ESG: Measure less, but better, p. 12.

both conceptually ambitious and rich in detail, shall be seen in this context. With its initial focus on "E" and climate urgency in particular, it seems to have the right initial focus, while at the same understanding the importance of "S" and "G", thus trying to give them proper consideration when setting the standard for what qualifies as "sustainable investment." The European regulatory approach to the topic seems to be reflecting the cutting-edge of sustainable finance market expert insights that while "the last 10–15 years have been about the impact of environmental and social issues on a portfolio", "the next ten years will be as much about the impact of investment on the environment."[10]

An important critical observation and proposal has been recently made in a Financial Times opinion piece that "ESG must be split in two"[11]: "ESG input" and "ESG output" approaches. While the European approach to regulating the field of sustainable finance leaves room for this important conceptual nuance and differentiation within SFDR's product-related disclosures regime, this new regulatory regime's definitions of "sustainable finance" and "sustainable investment" at the same time make clear that it generally understands these concepts as "ESG output" approaches.

With an intensive timeline in implementing the detailed and complex technical standard yet awaiting the test of practice, it remains to be seen if the entire machine of the new sustainable finance framework architecture will pass the test of practice. The same applies to the ambition to address such grand themes as improving market efficiency and contributing to the effort of ensuring that we not only make the world a better place now, but also ensure that the interests of the next generation are properly taken into account and considered.

---

[10] The Economist Special Report, Rating agencies: The signal and the noise, p. 10, quoting Michael Jantzi, the founder of Sustainalytics, an ESG research firm.

[11] *Kirk*.

List of References

Alexander, Kern: Principles of Banking Regulation, Cambridge (UK) 2019.

Ben-Shahar, Omri/*Schneider*, Carl E.: More Than You Wanted to Know, The Failure of Mandated Disclosure, Princeton 2014.

Brandeis, Louis D.: Other People's Money, And How Bankers Use it, New York 1913.

Carney, Mark: Value(s), Building a Better World for All, London 2021 (cit. *Carney*, Value(s)).

Carney, Mark: How We Get What We Value, BBC Reith Lectures, Episodes 1–4, December 2020 (available at: <https://www.bbc.co.uk/programmes/m000py8t>, last visited on January 15, 2023) (cit. *Carney*, How We Get What We Value).

The Economist: Special Report, ESG investing, Special Report, July 23rd–29th 2022 (available at: <https://www.economist.com/special-report/2022-07-23>, last visited on January 15, 2023).

Gehne, Katja: Nachhaltige Entwicklung als Rechtsprinzip, Tübingen 2011.

Kahl, Wolfgang: Nachhaltigkeitsverfassung, Tübingen: 2019.

Kirk, Stuart: ESG must be split in two, in: Financial Times, September 2, 2022 (available at: <https://www.ft.com/content/4d5ab95e-177e-42d6-a52f-572cdbc2eff2>, last visited on January 15, 2023).

Mathis, Klaus: Nachhaltige Entwicklung und Generationengerechtigkeit, Eine interdisziplinäre Studie aus rechtlicher, ökonomischer und philosophischer Sicht, Tübingen 2017.

Ross, Verena: Key priorities for EU retail fund investors, Speech at the Irish Funds Annual Global Funds Conference 2022, 31 May 2022 (available at: <https://www.esma.europa.eu/sites/default/files/library/esma34-466-284_verena_ross_speech_-_irish_funds_2022.pdf>, last visited on January 15, 2023).

Schoenmaker, Dirk/*Schramade*, Willem: Principles of Sustainable Finance, Oxford (UK) 2019.

Silvola, Hanna/*Landau*, Tiina: Sustainable Investing: Beating the Market with ESG, Basingstoke 2021.

Simmons & Simmons: SFDR, regulatory technical standards (RTS) published, Top 10 talking points, April 2022 (available at: <https://www.simmons-simmons.com/en/publications/cl1qklcg61r6c0a67rbt3x98o/esg-new-simmons-client-note-on-the-sfdr-rts>, last visited on January 15, 2023).

Zukas, Tadas/*Trafkowski*, Uwe: Sustainable Finance, The Regulatory Concept of Greenwashing under EU Law, in: Zeitschrift für Europarecht, Vol. 2/2022.

Laws, Regulations, Official Documents

Council of the EU: New rules on corporate sustainability reporting: provisional political agreement between the Council and the European Parliament (Press release updated on 30 June 2022 to include a link to the text following approval by Coreper), Press release, 21 June 2022 (available at: <https://www.consilium.europa.eu/en/press/press-releases/2022/06/21/new-rules-on-sustainability-disclosure-provisional-agreement-between-council-and-european-parliament/>, last visited on January 15, 2023) (cit. EU Council Press Release on CSRD 6/2022).

ESMA: Supervisory briefing, Sustainability risks and disclosures in the area of investment management, 31 May 2022 (available at: <https://www.esma.europa.eu/document/supervisory-briefing-sustainability-risks-and-disclosures-in-area-investment-management>, last visited on January 15, 2023) (cit. ESMA supervisory briefing 5/2022).

ESMA: Sustainable Finance Roadmap 2022–2024, 10 February 2022 (cit. ESMA Roadmap 2022).

European Commission: Questions related to Regulation (EU) 2019/2088 of the European Parliament and of the Council of 27 November 2019 on sustainability-related disclosures in the financial services sector (SFDR), May 17, 2022 (cit. SFDR/TR Q&A 5/2022).

European Commission: EC Q&A on sustainability-related disclosures, Question[s] related to Regulation (EU) 2019/2088 of the European Parliament and of the Council of 27 November 2019 on sustainability-related disclosures in the financial services sector (Sustainable Finance Disclosure Regulation 2019/2088), Ref. Ares(2021)4556843, July 14, 2021 (cit. SFDR Q&A 7/2021).

European Commission: Communication from the Commission to the European Parliament, the European Council, the Council, the European Central Bank, the European Economic and Social Committee and the Committee of the Regions, Strategy for Financing the Transition to a Sustainable Economy, COM/2021/390 final, Strasbourg, July 6, 2021 (cit. Sustainable Finance Strategy).

European Commission: Proposal for a Directive of the European Parliament and of the Council amending Directive 2013/34/EU, Directive 2004/109/EC, Directive 2006/43/EC and Regulation (EU) No 537/2014, as regards corporate sustainability reporting, COM(2021) 189 final, 2021/0104 (COD), Brussels, April 21, 2021, including Explanatory memorandum (cit. CSRD proposal draft 4/2021, CSRD proposal, or CSRD draft).

European Commission: Questions and Answers, Corporate Sustainability Reporting Directive proposal, Brussels, April 21, 2021 (cit. EC Q&A CSRD proposal draft 4/2021).

European Commission: Communication from the Commission to the European Parliament, the European Council, the Council, the European Central Bank, the European Economic and Social Committee and the Committee of the Regions, Action Plan, Financing Sustainable Growth, COM/2018/097 final, Brussels, March 8, 2018 (cit. Sustainable Finance Action Plan or Action Plan).

Deutsches Institut für Wirtschaftsforschung (Eds.)

Finance Meets Sustainability: A New Hope?

It is hoped that the financial sector will contribute significantly to the achievement of sustainability goals. The financial sector converts money in place, term, size and risk. It determines which projects are financed, influencing both the nature and return of funded projects. In principle, this decision power could be used to accelerate the transition to a sustainable economy. However, the crucial question is whether the financial sector can meet these high expectations?

The contributions in this edition of the *Vierteljahrshefte zur Wirtschaftsforschung* revolve around this question. The authors discuss the sustainability of dis-investment decisions, suggest a concept to measure sustainability in the real estate sector, examine if young adults are literate with respect to sustainable finance, and investigate whether green public procurement affects the financing of companies.

Vierteljahrshefte zur Wirtschaftsforschung, Volume 4/2021
tab., fig., 99 pages, 2022
ISBN 978-3-428-18652-5, € 84,90
Title also available as an e-book.

www.duncker-humblot.de

Printed by Libri Plureos GmbH
in Hamburg, Germany